The Smithsonian Guides to Natural America

CENTRAL APPALACHIA

CENTRAL APPALACHIA
TENNESSEE – KENTUCKY
WEST VIRGINIA

THE SMITHSONIAN GUIDES TO NATURAL AMERICA

CENTRAL APPALACHIA

WEST VIRGINIA, KENTUCKY, AND TENNESSEE

TEXT

Bruce Hopkins

PHOTOGRAPHY

Willard Clay and Kathy Clay

PREFACE

Thomas E. Lovejoy

SMITHSONIAN BOOKS • WASHINGTON, D.C.
RANDOM HOUSE • NEW YORK, N.Y.

Front cover: Fall Creek Falls State Park, Tennessee
Half-title page: Catawba rhododendron, Roan Mountain, Tennessee
Frontispiece: Little River, Great Smoky Mountains National Park
Back cover: Barred owl; rose-crested orchid; black bear cubs

THE SMITHSONIAN INSTITUTION
SECRETARY I. Michael Heyman
COUNSELOR TO THE SECRETARY FOR BIODIVERSITY
AND ENVIRONMENTAL AFFAIRS Thomas E. Lovejoy
ACTING DIRECTOR, SMITHSONIAN INSTITUTION PRESS Daniel H. Goodwin
SMITHSONIAN BOOKS
ACTING EDITOR IN CHIEF Alexis Doster III
MARKETING MANAGER Susan E. Romatowski
THE SMITHSONIAN GUIDES TO NATURAL AMERICA
SERIES EDITOR Sandra Wilmot
MANAGING EDITOR Ellen Scordato
SERIES PHOTO EDITOR Mary Jenkins
PHOTO EDITOR Sarah Longacre
ART DIRECTOR Mervyn Clay
ASSISTANT PHOTO EDITOR Ferris Cook
ASSISTANT PHOTO EDITOR Rebecca Williams
ASSISTANT EDITOR Seth Ginsberg
COPY EDITORS Kathryn Clark, Karen Hammonds, Claire Wilson
FACT CHECKER Jean Cotterell
PRODUCTION DIRECTOR Katherine Rosenbloom
Edward Bowen provided invaluable assistence on this volume.

Library of Congress Cataloging-in-Publication Data
Hopkins, Bruce.
    The Smithsonian guides to natural America. Central Appalachia—
West Virginia, Kentucky, and Tennessee/ text by Bruce Hopkins;
photographs by Willard Clay; preface by Thomas E. Lovejoy
        p. cm.
    Includes bibliographical references and index.
    ISBN 0-679-76474-7 (pbk.)
    1. Natural history—West Virginia—Guidebooks. 2. Natural
history—Kentucky—Guidebooks. 3. Natural history—Tennessee
—Guidebooks. 4. West Virginia—Guidebooks 5. Kentucky
—Guidebooks. 6. Tennessee—Guidebooks. II. Clay, Willard. II. Title.
QH105.W4H66 1996   95-9040
508.76—dc20   CIP
Manufactured in the United States of America
98765432

How to Use This Book

The Smithsonian Guides to Natural America explore and celebrate the preserved and protected natural areas of this country that are open for the public to use and enjoy. From world-famous national parks to tiny local preserves, the places featured in these guides offer a splendid panoply of this nation's natural wonders.

Divided by state and region, this book offers suggested itineraries for travelers, briefly describing the high points of each preserve, refuge, park, or wilderness area along the way. Each site was chosen for a specific reason: Some are noted for their botanical, zoological, or geological significance, others simply for their exceptional scenic beauty.

Information pertaining to the area as a whole can be found in the introductory sections to the book and to each chapter. In addition, specialized maps at the beginning of each book and chapter highlight an area's geography and geological features as well as pinpoint the specific locales that the author describes.

For quick reference, places of interest are set in **boldface** type; those set in **boldface** followed by the symbol ❖ are listed in the Site Guide at the back of the book. (This feature begins on page 263, just before the index.) Here, noteworthy sites are listed alphabetically by state, and each entry provides practical information that visitors need: telephone numbers, mailing addresses, and specific services available.

Addresses and telephone numbers of national, state, and local agencies and organizations are also listed. Also in appendices are a glossary of pertinent scientific terms and designations used to describe natural areas; the author's recommendations for further reading (both nonfiction and fiction); and a list of sources that can aid travelers planning a guided visit.

The words and images of these guides are meant to help both the active naturalist and the armchair traveler to appreciate more fully the environmental diversity and natural splendor of this country. To ensure a successful visit, always contact a site in advance to obtain detailed maps, updated information on hours and fees, and current weather conditions. Many areas maintain a fragile ecological balance. Remember that their continued vitality depends in part on responsible visitors who tread the land lightly.

C O N T E N T S

PREFACE

Central Appalachia is one of natural America's best kept se-crets. Here, where north and south meet in a seemingly incomprehensible jumble, the landscape can be a dramatic mix of gorges, plateaus, and mist-enshrouded mountains—or simply a heart-stopping green. It is home to the tulip tree, a source of perpetual fascination to me, with its springtime cuplike flowers of pastel yellow and pale red set against broad leaves of an exquisitely delicate green.

The brooding Appalachian Mountains were a barrier to westward expansion by European settlers until the mid-eighteenth century. Then Dr. Thomas Walker, and subsequently the better-known pioneer Daniel Boone, traversed the Cumberland Gap, opening a major gateway to the West. The lands beyond nourished herds of bison and elk and sky-darkening flocks of passenger pigeons. The last of those billions of birds, an individual by the name of Martha, died in the Cincinnati Zoo in 1914. Today, suitably preserved, Martha can be seen in the Smithsonian's National Museum of Natural History, poignant testimony to a time when natural resources were viewed as limitless.

Nonetheless, in West Virginia, Kentucky, and Tennessee, abundant opportunities for outdoor recreation remain, and while a few wildlife elements have disappeared, a great richness of flora and fauna await the persevering naturalist. Great Smoky Mountains National Park—America's most visited—is home to 27 species of salamanders, one of which, the red-cheeked, occurs nowhere else on earth. The same can be said of an evening primrose in West Virginia's shale barrens. Central Appalachia is also rhododendron and magnolia country; in addition, snow

---

PRECEDING PAGES: *In Kentucky's Cumberland Falls State Resort Park, vividly colored hardwoods surround huge boulders along the Cumberland River.*

buntings, usually northern residents, have been seen (and probably will be again) on Roan Mountain, and two forms of that wonderful gliding pixie, the flying squirrel, enliven the night.

The true faunal glories of Central Appalachia are the denizens of its grand aquatic systems. The region's rivers are so modified, in particular by the Tennessee Valley Authority, that some species are gone and others cling precariously, but even today one can catch glimpses here of some of the great aquatic faunas of the Americas. Especially fascinating to me are the freshwater mollusks, once the basis of a thriving industry that drilled buttons from their shells. It may be easy to ridicule the whimsical common names of these bivalves—pig toe, washboard, pink mucket pearly, and orange-footed pimpleback mussels, to name a few—but for those who are willing to take a closer look, these shoal- and riffle-dwellers are both lustrous and wondrous.

Although this region has been largely stripped of its original Native American population, their silent testimony endures. Behind the facade of modern America, evidence of their lives can still be seen. The rock houses of Kentucky's Red River Gorge are undeniable manifestations of their past presence. So too is the Trail of Tears, a national historic trail and an unsettling monument to the eviction of the Cherokee from their ancestral lands, protested by then-Congressman Davy Crockett.

Beyond the mountain and the ridge and valley, and then beyond the plateau country, lie the great river valleys. There nature has been greatly modified by human activity, particularly in the hardwood bottomland forests, which, along with the prairies, are now among the rarest of natural communities in North America. Yet here and there, such as at the Hatchie National Wildlife Refuge in Tennessee, one can still experience such forests firsthand.

OVERLEAF: *The American lotus, with its fragrant yellow flowers, blankets portions of the Mississippi River in western Kentucky and Tennessee.*

Here, too, is classic John J. Audubon country—and Wendell Berry territory as well. Its geography calls to mind such historic explorers and naturalists as Jim Bowie and John Muir, who in 1867 hiked a thousand miles in Tennessee. This region benefits even today from the noble efforts of the Civilian Conservation Corps of the 1930s and more recently from the visionary efforts of the Nature Conservancy.

Central Appalachia is, in the end, an area of extraordinary natural richness, all of it much closer to hand than most realize: the New River—not new at all—with white water that can rank with the best natural America has to offer; Land Between the Lakes, which I had the honor to dedicate as an international biosphere reserve in 1991 and where I first saw the rare red wolf; Reelfoot Lake, created by a major earthquake in 1811–12; spectacular Mammoth Cave, with 400 miles of passages and 4,000 other caves as well; and the Shenandoah and Tennessee valleys.

In this region are found the tallest waterfall in the United States, the most extensive virgin forest in the eastern United States, and the diverse habitats and species of Ice Mountain. Here, one can see krummholz vegetation at West Virginia's Dolly Sods, where the wind causes trees not just to bend but to actually move—and, when the weather and the moon are just right, an extraordinary rarity, the luminous moonbow at Cumberland Falls in Corbin, Kentucky. This volume about natural America has not only enlightened me about how much there is to enjoy in Central Appalachia but also, as it will you, made me yearn to go.

—Thomas E. Lovejoy
Counselor to the Secretary for
Biodiversity and Environmental Affairs,
SMITHSONIAN INSTITUTION

LEFT: *In Kentucky's Daniel Boone National Forest, a trail curves under Grays Arch along Red River Gorge where water and wind have eroded the soft stone into spectacular tunnels, natural bridges, and arches.*

CENTRAL APPALACHIA

50 0 50 Miles

50 0 50 Kilometers

INDIANA

ILLINOIS

MISSOURI

MISSISSIPPI R.

KENTUCKY

Louisville

FRANKFORT

Lexington

London

Paducah

Bowling
Green

Tennessee River

Cumberland River

Nashville

Cumberland Plateau

AR.

Jackson

TENNESSEE

Tennessee River

Memphis

Chattanooga

MISSISSIPPI

ALABAMA

INTRODUCTION

INTRODUCTION:
CENTRAL APPALACHIA

Like close-knit siblings, West Virginia, Kentucky, and Tennessee exhibit many similarities. The Appalachian Mountains cross them all, and major rivers flow through each, often forming their common borders. The three states were carved from the core of a huge, bountiful territory where Shawnee, Cherokee, and other Native Americans hunted and traded and where some of them lived. To European settlers all these lands were the frontier, left mostly unexplored until the mid-1700s, when Thomas Walker and then Daniel Boone made it over the rugged Appalachians, opening the way for the thousands of pioneers seeking the Eden of the West.

Geographically and culturally, this trio can be labeled neither northern nor southern—although many residents would claim them to be one or the other depending on what part of the region they call home. Along with Maryland, Delaware, and Missouri, they often are classified as the Border States, an ultimately imprecise term given their divergent histories. During the Civil War, western Virginia broke away from Confederate Virginia to become a state in the Union; Tennessee joined the Confederacy, although a sizable portion of its population, especially in the east, sympathized with the other side; and Kentucky stayed in the Union but essentially tried to remain neutral. (Kentucky's dual nature is symbolized by its status as the birthplace of both Abraham Lincoln and Jefferson Davis.)

To the geologist and the geographer, 100 percent of West Virginia and only about 30 percent of Kentucky and Tennessee are, strictly speaking, Appalachian. To less precise observers, however, these states deserve to be called the heart and soul of Appalachia, for all three share the mountains and are a delightful mix of North and South, both biologically and culturally. And despite their differences, the commonalities—especially the mountains—prevail.

PRECEDING PAGES: *A morning fog cloaks both sides of the autumn-hued Appalachians in Cumberland Gap National Historical Park, which includes the mountain pass where Daniel Boone first crossed into the West.*

The Appalachian Mountains stretch in a southwesterly direction for 1,200 miles from Newfoundland to Alabama. They do not form one continuous line but congregate in bunches—sometimes parallel, sometimes at right angles. Imagine a bed of wet cement. Spread your fingers and run them through the cement from northeast to southwest. Now, wiggle them here and there across the ruts and ridges. The Appalachians look something like that when seen from the air.

Ranging in width from 75 to 150 miles, the Appalachians are generally 2,000 to 5,000 feet in elevation, with some peaks and ridges as low as 1,000 feet and quite a few others higher than 6,000 feet. Although small by western U.S. standards, they are remnants of ancient peaks that may have been the highest in North America, as tall as today's Alps.

These mountains are not the result of one geological event but of several. Simply put, they comprise three distinct geological provinces, or zones, from east to west: the Blue Ridge, the ridge and valley, and the plateau. The Blue Ridge is the oldest, with metamorphic and igneous rocks formed in the first of what may have been several collisions of geologic plates that contained the continents and smaller pieces, or islands. In the three states covered in this book, these ancient Blue Ridge mountains can be seen near Harpers Ferry at the end of West Virginia's eastern Panhandle and in the Unakas and Great Smoky Mountains of Tennessee.

The ridge-and-valley zone contains folded and upthrusted sedimentary rocks that run in every direction. Generally the ridges consist of relatively harder sandstones, and the valleys of softer limestones and shales that have been eaten away by erosion. The ridge-and-valley Appalachians stretch west and southwest of Martinsburg in West Virginia and west of the Unakas and Smokies in Tennessee. The large valley just west of the Blue Ridge, known in West Virginia and Virginia as the Shenandoah Valley and in Tennessee as the Tennessee Valley or the Great Valley of East Tennessee, is a major feature of this zone.

The plateau zone consists of sedimentary layers that were lifted but not intensely folded by continental collisions and thus are still mostly horizontal. But do not be misled by that statement, for much of the plateau, especially the eastern portion, is not flat but rugged and highly eroded, with steep, twisting gorges. A visitor soon discovers that flat is a relative term in the Appalachians, where ridges and rounded hills can leave hikers or motorists wondering why it's called a plateau and when the next so-called flat valley will appear. The plateau zone of the Appalachian Mountains covers the remainder of central and western West Virginia, where it is known as the Allegheny Plateau, and roughly the eastern third of both Kentucky and Tennessee, where it is called the Cumberland Plateau. The mountains within the plateaus are known respectively as the Alleghenies and the Cumberlands.

The land descends toward the Mississippi west of the plateau: in Kentucky to the Bluegrass area, the Knobs, the Pennyrile, the Western Kentucky Coal Field, and the Gulf Coastal Plain; in Tennessee to the Nashville Basin, Highland Rim, and Gulf Coastal Plain. These areas of lesser elevation were created in ancient times when an inland sea covered an enormous area that extended north from the Gulf of Mexico as far as St. Louis.

Unlike many of the western U.S. mountain ranges, the Appalachians have deep soils that support lush vegetation, and even the peaks and ridgetops in these three states are usually forested. The only exceptions are balds, found on a few of the highest peaks and on certain ridges and slopes where the terrain has been denuded, probably the result of logged or mined lands that have not been reforested or have not recovered on their own.

The Ice Age affected this region significantly even though the continental glaciers only touched what are now the northernmost boundaries of West Virginia and Kentucky. As the glaciers advanced and the climate cooled, northern species were pushed south. When the glaciers melted, many northern species stayed on, seeking refuge in the cooler temperatures of the higher elevations and leaving the lower areas to the native southern species. Today most of the Appalachians in these three states are a textbook transitional zone, with a good mix of oaks and hickories typical of the northern forests as well as more typically southern species such as the yellow poplar (also called tulip tree), pine, rhododendron, azalea, and even the occasional magnolia. Prime examples of the mingling of these species can be seen at Roan Mountain and in the Great Smoky Mountains, both in Tennessee. Naturalist Maurice Brooks once observed a flock of snow buntings on Roan Mountain's balds that were eating the white, three-toothed cinquefoil, the same plant they feed on in Canada's Gaspé Peninsula.

RIGHT: *In early spring a redbud tree flaunts its delicate pink blossoms against the exposed sedimentary layers of West Virginia's New River Gorge. Continental collisions did not buckle the ancient formations here.*

6

ABOVE: *Purple violets pop up through gray lichens at Land Between the Lakes, which straddles the border of Kentucky and Tennessee. This international biosphere reserve protects more than 800 floral species.*

The birds had flown in severe weather, bypassing heavily forested areas, to find their little bit of Canada and food.

Although pockets remain, most of the region's virgin forests were destroyed by logging or mining operations. However, efforts to reforest the lands have been fairly extensive and successful, especially in the national forests, which carry names associated with our Native American and pioneer heritage: Monongahela, Daniel Boone, and Cherokee.

The climate varies from state to state, with West Virginia having fairly cool to cold winters and hot, humid summers. Except in the mountains, Kentucky and Tennessee have mild winters and warm to hot summers, and spring and fall tend to be pleasant, with mild days and cool nights. All three get an average of 40 to 45 inches of precipitation a year, although the high mountainous areas receive much more, especially in late winter and spring. The highest peaks in the Smokies get as much as 80 inches of precipitation in rain and snow.

ABOVE: *Ubiquitous throughout the three central Appalachian states, white-tailed deer prefer brushy areas and woodlands. At dawn and dusk they browse on leaves, grasses, and other low-growing plants.*

Not surprisingly, an endless number of creeks, streams, and rivers crisscross the region, including such major waterways as the New, Kanawha, Monongahela, Kentucky, Cumberland, Tennessee, Ohio, and Mississippi rivers.

The eastern edge of the Appalachian Plateau is generally the eastern Continental Divide, a line separating river systems that flow east to the Atlantic from those heading west to the Mississippi. Because most of the precipitation falls to the west, most of the runoff waters flow into the Atlantic via the Gulf of Mexico rather than through the Chesapeake Bay. Virginia's Shenandoah River, which is fed by tributaries along West Virginia's eastern border, takes the Chesapeake route to the Atlantic by flowing north and merging with the Potomac River at Harpers Ferry. On

OVERLEAF: *In western Kentucky, velvety green duckweed floats among the motionless gossamer reflections of bald cypresses at one of the 11 lakes in the Ballard County Wildlife Management Area, near the Ohio River.*

9

the other hand, the New River, which starts southeast of the plateau in North Carolina, follows the Ohio-Mississippi path to the sea.

Although Tennessee's Reelfoot Lake, which appeared after an earthquake in 1811–12, is the only large natural lake in the three states, there are plenty of artificial lakes created by hydroelectric-power and flood-control dams on major rivers. Many of these manmade lakes have become havens for natural life, especially birds, and many of them are surrounded today by woodlands and forests that attract deer, foxes, wild turkeys, and plenty of other wildlife. Do not completely discount these lake areas despite their emphasis on recreation.

Spring and fall are the best times to visit most of the places mentioned in this book; the crowds are not as large as in the summer, and the humidity is lower. Each season, however, has special attributes to recommend it. Spring brings lush flowering shrubs and vibrant wildflowers, burgeoning creeks and plunging waterfalls, and emerging frogs, toads, and salamanders. Fall delivers enormous flocks of migrating birds, colorful autumn foliage, and golden, temperate days. Summer is summer, but most of the streams still run full, at least in the east, and vegetation is verdant and flourishing. Winter in the higher elevations appeals to those who treasure privacy and like to follow animal tracks in the snow, and winter in the mild lower elevations has its own stark allure.

Some state parks have the word "resort" in their names—officially in Kentucky and unofficially in West Virginia and Tennessee. In Kentucky it simply means the park has a lodge; in West Virginia and Tennessee it signifies the park has a golf course, lodge, and probably cabins or cottages. Some have swimming pools and other recreational facilities. Only the most ardent environmentalists, backpackers, and ascetics should avoid these resorts; most of them have interesting natural features and lightly used trails—plus hot meals and showers!

Although this book focuses on natural areas, travelers should take the time to stop at a few historic sites to get a sense of each state's human history. A partial list of prominent figures—besides the aforementioned Walker, Lincoln, and Davis—includes Davy Crockett, Sam Houston, John James Audubon, James Polk, Andrew Jackson, Thomas "Stonewall" Jackson, Sequoyah, Booker T. Washington, Pearl Buck, Patricia Neal, and

LEFT: *Gamely growing out of a jagged, lichen-encrusted rock, a flowering mountain laurel adds a touch of bright pink to an eroded, upthrusted cliff in Tennessee's Great Smoky Mountains National Park.*

Loretta Lynn. All three states claim Daniel Boone in one way or another, and the word Cumberland is ubiquitous in Tennessee and Kentucky, recalling the name of the gap discovered by that pioneer explorer and adventurer. Let serendipity be your guide in matters historic and cultural.

And finally, a practical tip: Motorists should not wait until the last minute to buy gasoline. In many areas service stations are few and far between. A wrong or missed turn in the mountains can get you lost quickly, and being both lost and out of gas more than doubles your problems. Be especially aware of this in the three mammoth national forests, where many roads, sites, and features are not well marked. Fill up and then confidently take the secondary and the primitive dirt and gravel roads, for they offer some of the best opportunities to really see the countryside and its special features. Of course, the interstate highways are a great help if there are many miles between sites and your time is limited.

The itineraries in the following pages describe two tours for each state. The book starts in the far eastern corner of West Virginia's Eastern Panhandle and proceeds from east to west in West Virginia and Kentucky, and west to east in Tennessee. Any of the sites noted in this volume, however, can derail a traveler's prearranged schedule. In any park or other preserve, one turn leads beguilingly to the next, one hilltop issues a challenge to gaze upon what is just out of sight, and each sight or sound of wildlife promises additional fulfillment if one but tarries a moment longer. Thus each loop is a suggestion. Look at the maps and jump in at any convenient point, visit a few sites, backtrack if you like, and do not overlook the possibility of crossing state borders and linking tour loops or making up your own tour. And for heaven's sake, do not try to do the whole circuit through all three states in one trip! You would end up as bug-eyed as a writer sitting at a computer for a month. Happy trails.

RIGHT: *A strikingly patterned eastern black swallowtail feeds on bright yellow and white honeysuckle blossoms. Eschewing the woods, this butterfly species prefers the openness of meadows, farmlands, and streambeds.*

WEST VIRGINIA

PART ONE

W E S T   V I R G I N I A

Political boundaries and geography make strange bedfellows: That truism is illustrated by the shapes of many states, but no example is more striking than that of West Virginia. If it were described only by its extremities, the Mountain State would seem to be the size of Texas. It possesses boundaries farther north than Pittsburgh, farther east than Rochester, farther south than Richmond, and almost as far west as Detroit. Yet, among the nation's 50 states, this seeming behemoth ranks 41st in area, with only 24,231 square miles. In fact, its narrow northern and eastern panhandles account for much of the misconception—besides giving the state a shape like a frog with its rear legs splayed.

All of West Virginia lies within the Appalachians, known as the Alleghenies in this state. The towering ancestral Appalachians were gradually eroded by water and wind, so for a period West Virginia was marked more by low plains than high peaks. A later mountain-building episode caused by the closing of the seafloor of the ancestral Atlantic Ocean created another upheaval during which great blocks of the plains were thrust upward, setting off another sequence of erosion that accounts for much of today's rugged terrain.

Geologists believe that some rivers, such as the New, follow parts of the route of the ancient Teays River, the mighty flow that crossed the eastern half of the continent before the Ice Age. Thus, some riverbeds are older than the mountains through which they wander. New River Gorge, cut down into ancient formations that have long since disappeared from the surface, is 1,500 feet deep in places.

Much more recently, from about 70,000 to 10,000 years ago, West Virginia was approached so closely by Ice Age glaciers that it became a refuge for many species associated with the northern United States and Canada, a refrain the traveler will hear cited at countless parks and preserves throughout the Central Appalachians.

PRECEDING PAGES: *Along West Virginia's Highland Scenic Highway, brilliant fall foliage accentuates the receding ridges of the Appalachians.*

The western part of the state generally has more gentle, folded layers of rocks than the sharp, higher peaks and ridges of the east. West Virginia's mean elevation is 1,480 feet, the highest of all states east of the Mississippi River. Elevations range from 240 feet at Harpers Ferry to 4,861 feet at Spruce Knob, not to be confused with the shorter Big Spruce Knob, both of which are in Monongahela National Forest.

Mean temperatures for the state range from 56 degrees Fahrenheit in the southwestern counties to 48 degrees in the mountains. The eastern panhandle tends to be warmer, because it is close enough to the coast to be influenced by the Atlantic Ocean. Likewise, annual rainfall varies from more than 50 inches at the highest points to 35 to 40 inches in the eastern panhandle. The state as a whole gets an average of four inches of rain each month, and because it has so many steep and narrow valleys, flash floods are a constant threat. High mountainous areas have received as much as 100 inches of snow in a year.

The abrupt successions of sheer ridges and valleys are also the reason why this region remained essentially inaccessible for settlement until the early 1700s. Although Shawnee, Iroquois, and Delaware peoples had been hunting and trading in the area for years, few of them lived here permanently. Rivers and gaps played major roles in what European settlement did occur later. Many of the first pioneers came not from Virginia but from Pennsylvania, Maryland, and Delaware, starting at the Harpers Ferry gap and traveling through the Shenandoah Valley. Some came from the north and settled on the northeast border along the Potomac, others floated down the Ohio River on the western border and set down roots in such places as Wheeling and Parkersburg. The Monongahela and the Kanawha, major tributaries of the Ohio, attracted still others. Even so, West Virginia remained sparsely populated until after the Civil War, when the advent of railroads sparked a rash of widespread logging and mining.

Coal was and is the big attraction, and West Virginia ranks second only to Kentucky in the production of bituminous coal. To accommodate the mining industry, virtually all of the mountains and hillsides were heavily logged. A few stands of virgin forest remain today, but some of the state's most striking characteristics—windy mountain balds and drowsy muskegs—are at least partially the result of the denuding and burning of mountaintops once resplendent with hardwoods. Efforts to restore the forests began in the early 1900s, and today, thanks in large part to the extensive Monongahela National Forest, West Virginia is once again rich in natural beauty.

CHAPTER ONE

EASTERN
WEST VIRGINIA:
LOWEST POINT, HIGHEST PEAK

Thomas Jefferson, one of America's early naturalists, said that viewing the confluence of the Potomac and Shenandoah rivers at Harpers Ferry was "worth a voyage across the Atlantic." "You stand on a very high point of land," he wrote in his *Notes on Virginia*. "On your right comes up the Shenandoah, having ranged along the foot of the mountain an hundred miles to see a vent. On your left approaches the Patowmac, in quest of a passage also. In the moment of their junction they rush together against the mountain, rend it asunder, and pass off to the sea."

Harpers Ferry, indeed, is a good place to begin a voyage through eastern West Virginia, for here the Blue Ridge, the oldest of the Appalachian Mountains, touches a corner of West Virginia across from Maryland, and from here the ridge extends south through Virginia into North Carolina and Tennessee.

In the eastern Panhandle, this itinerary moves on to the beginnings of Alleghenies, with hot and cold visits respectively at Berkeley Springs and mysterious Ice Mountain. Then it heads north to a forest east of Morgantown and swings south to a mountain bog and a delightful cathedral of hemlocks.

Moving next into the heart of West Virginia's Alleghenies, the tour

LEFT: *Precipitous and massive, Seneca Rocks is one of the Monongahela National Forest's prime natural attractions, both for travelers motoring through and for intrepid rock climbers testing their skills.*

comes to the gigantic Monongahela National Forest and its many components, including several wilderness areas and separate state parks. This is a region of second-growth hardwood forests typical of those found throughout the mid-Appalachians, of numerous waterfalls, limestone caves, a river that disappears, spruce forests more commonly found in the North, and a touch of tundralike vegetation at a place called Dolly Sods.

This eastern tour loop takes in an impressive rock formation at Seneca Rocks and the state's highest peak, Spruce Knob, where the west wind can be bitingly cold in summer as well as in winter. To the south is Cranberry Glades, where various plants flourish in a mat-like sphagnum moss far from their usual northern locations.

This route leads back and forth, up and down the ridges, along valleys, and through small towns and hamlets. Be patient, for much of it is on country roads. Interstate highways are few and far between: There's one near Morgantown partway into the first tour, one at White Sulfur Springs at the end, and another at Bluefield, where the second West Virginia loop starts. But the point is to go slow and look around.

"There are two ways to look at mountains—from the lowlands below and from the heights themselves," Maurice Brooks wrote in *The Appalachians.* "The first has many advantages, of course. It is less taxing, and there is special appeal in a view that lifts our eyes skyward. Even such modest mountains as we find in much of Appalachia can loom large on the horizon. Those who stay in the lowlands, however, can have no real idea of the different world on the summits."

With that advice in mind, a traveler is best advised to get out of the car or van and walk some of the many trails cited in these pages to discover new worlds. Also, as Thoreau suggests, be like a camel and ruminate as you walk.

EASTERN PANHANDLE

Harpers Ferry National Historical Park❖, the easternmost point in the state, is better known for human than natural history. It was here, in an 1859 prelude to the Civil War, that abolitionist John Brown raided

---

OVERLEAF: *American painter Rembrandt Peale (1778–1860) captured the grandeur of Harpers Ferry, where the Shenandoah flows into the Potomac and West Virginia meets Maryland (left) and Virginia (right).*

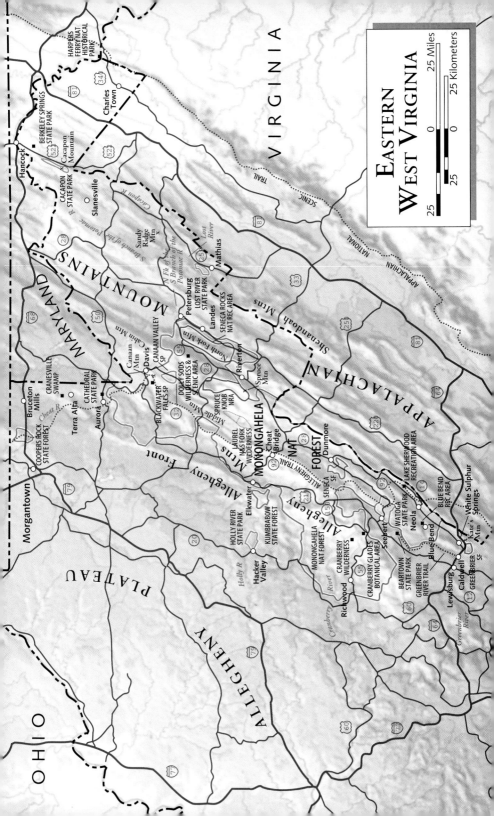

the arsenal established years before by George Washington. Although the elevation of the Blue Ridge on the south side of the Potomac at Harpers Ferry is only 1,180 feet, the ridge is relatively imposing because the elevation at the river is only 240 feet—the lowest point in the state.

Harpers Ferry National Historical Park has a few short trails, most of which are history oriented, but they're not without interest to the naturalist. The 2,144-mile **Appalachian National Scenic Trail❖** also reaches its midpoint near Harpers Ferry, and the Appalachian Trail Conference, which manages the trail for the National Park Service, has its headquarters here. The trail crosses the Potomac from Maryland on a footbridge and soon enters Virginia, touching West Virginia briefly again near Pearisburg, Virginia. The footbridge across the Potomac is also part of the towpath of the **Chesapeake and Ohio Canal National Historical Park,** which runs 184 miles between Cumberland, Maryland, and Washington, D.C. Harpers Ferry is located on Route 340 west of Frederick, Maryland, near Charles Town, West Virginia.

About 50 miles northwest of Harpers Ferry at the junction of Route 9 and Interstate 70 is one of the area's natural, albeit highly developed, attractions, **Berkeley Springs State Park❖.** Known to Native Americans and later promoted as a spa that had George Washington's patronage, the Berkeley Springs network of five key springs and many lesser springs discharges about 2,000 gallons of 74.3-degree-Fahrenheit water every minute. This is a place for both hikers and urbanites to soothe sore muscles.

About 10 miles south of Berkeley Springs, off Route 522, is Cacapon Mountain, 2,300 feet in elevation and the most prominent natural feature of **Cacapon State Park❖.** The 6,000-acre park has some 30 miles of hiking and cross-country skiing trails that climb 1,400 feet to the ridgeline and offer scenic views of forested hillsides broken by sandstone outcroppings.

An unusual dichotomy of climates and habitats marks the surroundings of the Nature Conservancy's property at **Ice Mountain❖,** along Route 127 near Slanesville. Within a distance of 500 feet and an elevation range of 75 feet, temperatures can vary from 38 degrees Fahrenheit in air currents created by underground ice formations to more than 100 degrees caused by intense reflection of the sun off steep shale barrens left by Ice Age glaciers.

Two theories attempt to explain the phenomenon of Ice Mountain. One says that although the glaciers did not descend into West Virginia, an ancient underlying ice formation has been gradually melting for thousands of years, giving off cool hillside breezes. The other theory is that a reservoir of ice is renewed annually by snow, sleet, and rain. Rare species that flourish in the coolness at Ice Mountain include the bristly rose, twinflower, and bunchberry. The evening primrose is endemic to the shale barrens. Arrangements to tour Ice Mountain must be made two weeks in advance through the Nature Conservancy's state headquarters in Charleston.

SOUTH FROM MORGANTOWN: MOUNTAIN BOGS AND HEMLOCKS

If time is not important, make the 100-mile trip to **Coopers Rock State Forest❖** by scenic Routes 50 west and 26 north. (A faster, more direct route is in Maryland via Interstate 68, which bisects the forest 8 miles west of Bruceton Mills and 12 miles east of Morgantown.) Travelers through middle and western West Virginia may find it hard to believe they are on a plateau. The highways, like the rivers, generally are deeply cut, so one is always looking up at hillsides and mountainsides. From Coopers Rock, it is possible to see that the lands to the west are more of a plateau than they first appear to be. To the east are the more rugged and dramatic folds of ridges and valleys.

At 12,700 acres, Coopers Rock is the largest state forest in West Virginia. Its name alludes to a fugitive cooper who hid in the forest for several years but continued to make and sell barrels. He certainly had spectacular views of the Cheat River 1,200 feet below. Fifty miles of trails meander through the forest, and one leads to a grove of hemlocks more than 300 years old. Another of the 16 trails visits an overlook at Raven Rock. More than half of the forest is managed for teaching and research by West Virginia University.

Naturalist Norma Jean Venable notes that a traveler once described the Nature Conservancy's **Cranesville Swamp❖** as "a cool, wet, and shrouded visit to a netherworld," and while wandering the bog's surrounding forest, the traveler may find the prosaic presence of white-tailed deer particularly reassuring in such otherworldly surroundings. About 30 miles southeast of Coopers Rock, off Route 47 north of Terra

ABOVE: *Sprouting in early spring, skunk cabbage exudes a rank scent to attract insects that assist in pollination.*

RIGHT: *Lacy ferns and woodland wildflowers carpet the understory of Cathedral State Park, but the aura created by the site's towering hemlocks and oaks inspired its name.*

Alta, Cranesville Swamp encompasses 600 acres with a network of creeks. Venable's booklet *Cranesville Swamp* explains that many plants and animals living in this high mountain bog "usually abide in more northern and boreal areas such as New England and Canada." Species left behind, or adrift, from their natural habitat are known as relicts—remnants from the Ice Age in this case.

Cranesville Swamp receives about 50 inches of rainfall annually and three times that much snow. Although most people associate swamps and bogs with low-lying, hot locales such as those along the Mississippi, Cranesville has an elevation of 2,900 feet, and sometimes snow lingers on the ground into the summer. The high amount of precipitation and the poor drainage in the clay and rocky soil help create this phenomenon.

More accurately called a bog, or muskeg, because it lacks the standing water that defines a true swamp, Cranesville can be traversed along a 2,500-foot boardwalk only inches above the matlike sphagnum moss. Push a finger lightly into the black muck, and the response is a slight, wet depression more reminiscent of muddy burlap than soil. Among the 200 plant species are cotton grass (a sedge), skunk cabbage, sundew, and large cranberries. The bog's acidity is not conducive to hardwoods or conifers, but an adjacent forest is home to red spruce, white pine, red maple, wild black cherry, hemlock, trembling aspen, and yellow birch. Here also is the southern extremity of the tamarack (eastern larch), a conifer that loses its leaves in the fall. Various ferns grow lushly to a height of several feet.

When one travels through West Virginia and parts of nearby states, there are moments when the word "cathedral" comes to mind, especially in conifer forests, with their overarching ceilings of branches, slanted, columnar sunlight, and relatively clear floors. This sense of a place of peace and reflection accounts for the name of **Cathedral State Park❖,** a 133-acre enclave along Route 50 immediately east of Aurora, about 7 miles south of Terra Alta. The park is beautiful on a fine, crisp wintry day, when fresh snow lays gently upon the boughs and a whisper of a breeze sends crystals twirling to the ground.

A succession of owners chose not to log this acreage, which thus survived as a virgin hemlock-dominated forest. Only the elimination of blighted chestnut trees was allowed. Brandon Haas, who had worked at the Brookside Hotel at the edge of the forest, sold it to the state in 1942 with the proviso that it be preserved in its pristine state. Today it remains so, altered only by gentle paths, directional signs, and footbridges over the gurgling, meandering Rhine Creek.

In 1966, Cathedral State Park was entered into the National Registry of Natural History Landmarks as an "area that possesses exceptional value in illustrating the natural history of the United States of America." In 1983, it was cited by the Society of American Foresters "as an out-

standing example of a vegetative community in a near natural condition ... with its associated biotic, edaphic, geologic, and aquatic features... dedicated for scientific and educational purposes."

The park's virgin stand of majestic eastern hemlock, the climax species here, is thought to be some 300 years old. The patriarch Centennial Hemlock measures 123 feet tall, has a trunk circumference of 18 feet, boasts a spread of nearly 70 feet, and is believed to be some 500 years old—a mere seedling when Columbus made his voyages. Hemlocks share the forest with more than a dozen other tree and shrub species, including American beech, white and red oaks, red maple, spruce, and rhododendron. In spring and summer wildflower species such as jack-in-the-pulpit, ladies' tresses, Canada violet, trailing arbutus, bluet, and wood anemone add their delicate colors to the woodlands as well. More than two dozen bird species, both gray and red foxes, deer, and fox squirrels have been seen here.

ABOVE: *A woodland denizen, the gray fox is a nocturnal creature and the only member of the canid family with an aptitude for climbing.*

LEFT: *The vast Monongahela National Forest covers 900,000 acres in eastern West Virginia. Here the autumn sun highlights golden grasses and American mountain ash near the Highland Scenic Highway.*

To Suzanne Lord and Jon Metzger, in *The West Virginia One-Day Trip Book,* the park seems "to bring a spiritual message: the inevitability of life's circle and a promise of rebirth." Cathedral is indeed a special little place.

TREASURES OF THE MONONGAHELA

Some regard the creation of the **Monongahela National Forest❖** as the beginning of responsible conservation in the area. Years of depleting the forest and gouging the earth for commercial purposes threatened the ecology of the state. Today the Monongahela's 900,000 protected acres stretch along West Virginia's eastern border with Virginia, and all

31

but 50,000 of those acres are in the Appalachian Mountains.

Throughout the length and breadth of the national forest are numerous marvels of nature—arresting rock formations, windy knolls where stunted trees fight to survive, roaring rivers and falls, deep gorges, and exotic muskegs. Some of the sites discussed below are administered by the U.S. Forest Service. Others are pockets within the forest managed by state or local agencies or other organizations.

For the ambitious hiker, a wonderful way to see many pieces of the Monongahela's treasure trove is to travel the 330-mile **Allegheny Trail❖** from northwest of Bruceton Mills on the Pennsylvania–West Virginia border to Peters Mountain. The trail links up with the Appalachian Trail in southeast West Virginia and passes through or near three state parks, four state forests, two designated national wilderness areas, and the **George Washington and Jefferson National Forests❖**. The Monongahela also has many historic sites, such as the Fairfax Stone, which marks both the western boundary of lands granted Lord Fairfax by the King of England and the traditional headwaters of the Potomac River. There is even an auto tour of Civil War sites.

In the northeastern section of the Monongahela, south of Davis on Route 29, lies **Blackwater Falls State Park❖**. Blackwater's history illustrates the destruction-to-preservation cycle undergone by many of America's forests. Thomas Jefferson's father once led an exploration party that found the woods here so forbidding as to merit the adjective "accursed," but in the late 1800s and early 1900s loggers virtually denuded the succulent hillsides. Today, the Blackwater area again is blessed with dense forests of spruce, hemlock, cherry, and maple, and it is doubtful anyone would regard them as accursed.

The wild Blackwater River takes its name from its darkish color, which comes from tannic acids leached from spruce and hemlock, plus the presence of iron oxide. While Blackwater Falls itself can be somewhat placid in seasons of drought, it generally roars as it plunges 63 feet. Throughout the 1,700-acre park, the river descends 560 feet, and overlooks provide spectacular views of the gorge with

---

RIGHT: *Plummeting some 60 feet into a rugged, intensely scenic gorge, Blackwater Falls makes itself heard before it is seen. Tannin from nearby spruce and hemlock trees often gives the water a dark cast.*

ABOVE: *In Dolly Sods Wilderness and Scenic Area, fall burnishes the wild blueberry shrubs that grow among the stone formations of*

its high exposures of rock and of two other falls, Elakala and Pendleton. Seventeen hiking and cross-country skiing trails that total about 18 miles wind throughout the park, and the Allegheny Trail passes through, exiting near Pendleton Lake.

High in the Alleghenies, off Route 32 south of Blackwater and Davis, is **Canaan Valley Resort❖,** a state park. At about 3,200 feet this is the highest major valley east of the Mississippi, separating Canaan Mountain (3,702 feet) on the west from Cabin Mountain (4,200 feet) on the east. In simplified terms, the existence of this wetland valley in the mountains is attributed to an insoluble combination of eroded limestone and minerals in the soil. Precipitation is abundant, with more than 53 inches of annual rainfall and snowfalls of up to 48 inches. One story holds that the Canaan (ca-NAINE) Valley was named by an eighteenth-century fur trader who gazed upon it from atop Cabin Mountain, likening it to the biblical promised land of

the Bear Rocks section. The berries, foliage, and twigs are forage for the numerous songbirds, small mammals, and deer on this high plateau.

Canaan. Like Cranesville Swamp and Dolly Sods Wilderness, the valley still supports relict boreal species left behind by Ice Age glaciers.

Humans, too, have left their mark on the valley by cutting down forests and inadvertently destroying a deep and nourishing humus with fire. According to naturalist Norma Jean Venable some fires were deliberately set in the hope that bluegrass could be grown on the land left bare by loggers. Often it was not bluegrass that recloaked the land however, but "briers, fire cherry, aspen, and bracken fern, vegetation . . . indicative of severe past land disturbance," she writes in her publication *Canaan Valley*. In fairness to our predecessors, some of the changes were wrought by the tree-felling and damming of industrious beavers.

Perhaps willy-nilly, these human and wildlife populations have contributed some variety to the state's natural habitats. Today wetlands make up only one percent of West Virginia, ranking it last in the nation—and Canaan Valley's nearly 7,000 acres along the meandering Blackwater

River account for nearly one tenth of this sparse ecological treasure.

Trails for hikers and cross-country skiers wind through various plant and tree communities, and a 7.8-mile trail connects Canaan Valley Resort and Blackwater Falls State Park. Of the some 523 plant species in the valley, 26 are rare. Moreover, 286 mammal, reptile, bird, fish, and amphibian species live within the forests, marshes, meadows, and waters. The trees include a stand of quaking and bigtooth aspens and groves of hawthorns. Rare animals include the Virginia northern flying squirrel, northern water shrew, Virginia big-eared bat, and southern bog lemming.

DOLLY SODS AND LOST RIVER

A sense of otherworldliness can accompany an initial trip to **Dolly Sods Wilderness and Scenic Area❖,** just east of Canaan Valley. Part of the Allegheny Front, the eastern edge of the Allegheny Plateau, Dolly Sods often is described as a displaced piece of arctic tundra, which, with its rocky plains and upland bogs, might be more at home in northern Canada. Grass balds and rugged deposits of broken rock abut slightly lower bogs and marshes, which are advancing through species succession and might become red spruce forests in time.

Throughout the southern Appalachians, balds (grassy, treeless areas atop mountains and on ridges and slopes) remain mysterious. Some people theorize that either natural fires or those purposely set by Native Americans to flush out game account for the sparseness of any vegetation more than a foot tall. Also known as sods, grass balds were used in pioneer times as grazing lands, and this particular location has been traced

ABOVE: *Ranging throughout the Alleghenies, in winter the snowshoe, or varying, hare molts from brown to white for camouflage and grows furry "snowshoes" to help it outrun predators.*

LEFT: *The lichen-covered boulders atop Dolly Sods glow in the setting sun. The bare rocks of this classic mountain bald seem ethereal, a stepping-off point to the heavens beyond.*

37

to a family named Dahle. In that imaginative combination of spelling and pronunciation that so enlivens American geography, the area eventually became known as Dolly Sods. Sections of the area were once heavily wooded, but in the late 1800s huge hemlocks and spruce were logged. As a result, the deep humus layer dried out and fires were able to burn it down to the rocks.

ABOVE: *One of the few poisonous snakes found in West Virginia, the copperhead, with its dark hourglass-shaped crossbands, frequents ravines and rocky, wooded hillsides.*

RIGHT: *Not just hanging out, three cubs and their protective mother take refuge above the ground. Unlike grizzlies, black bears climb trees to snack on twigs, foliage, and nuts—as well as to outwit bees for honey.*

OVERLEAF: *As the sun sets, the imposing Seneca Rocks formation glows a bright orange, accentuating the jagged edges of the ridge.*

In 1975 Congress set aside more than 10,000 acres here as a wilderness area, protecting it from significant alteration. To the east is a 2,400-acre scenic area, which is approached via Routes 24 and 11 southeast of Red Creek, although some roads are impassable in winter. In spring rhododendrons dot acres of rocks and boulders, mountain laurels put on a colorful show in June, and foot-high blueberry plants are lush with berries in July. The most distinctive appearance, however, belongs to the stunted red spruce, which have branches only on the side facing away from the withering westerly winds. With low, spreading boughs—they are often wider than they are tall—these red spruce rarely rise above ten feet. Battered, dignified, and scraggly, they look like infantry flags tattered from battle.

Featured at Dolly Sods are a bald covered in Allegheny fly-back (also called mountain oat grass), which takes on a whitish hue in the autumn, and the Northland Loop Bog, which has a short boardwalk. Fourteen trails cover more than 45 miles, and, true to the philosophy of wilderness management, crossings of Red Creek are left to the traveler's imagination and determination,

for no bridges are provided. "Wet and rocky" is a common description in the U.S. Forest Service's hiking guide.

Mammals here include beavers, six kinds of squirrels, bobcats, various weasels, shrews, mice, and voles. About 100 species of nesting and migratory birds have been sighted, and 70 ferns, flowers, and shrubs have been catalogued. In addition to the spruce, there are more than two dozen kinds of trees, including hemlocks, pines, black and yellow birches, maples, and the mountain ash, with its distinctive red berry clusters that contrast so strikingly with winter's heavy blanket of snow. Rapid changes of temperature and sudden storms can occur unexpectedly, and at 4,000 feet Dolly Sods can experience frost at any time of the year, even in summer. Temperatures drop below zero during the winter. Be prepared.

A trip out of the Monongahela National Forest reaches **Lost River State Park❖,** 25 miles southeast of Dolly Sods. Lying amid the hills and narrow valleys of the eastern part of the state, near the West Virginia portion of Virginia's **George Washington and Jefferson National Forests❖,** Lost River can be approached from the north via Route 259; at Mathias, take Route 12 west four miles to the park. The Lee family of Virginia used the area as a summer retreat in the early 1800s, and American Revolution general "Light-Horse Harry" Lee's cabin is now a park museum. Lost River State Park is named for a nearby river, which got its sobriquet because it slips underground at Sandy Ridge Mountain and reemerges three miles to the north as the Cacapon River. Howard's Lick Run, a tributary, flows through the heavily forested park, which has 19 trails that roam through 30 miles within its 3,700 acres. A spot known as Granny Crow, at 3,200 feet, provides views of the highlands.

The black bear heads a list of about 50 animal species found here, including five types of bats, bobcat, copperheads, and five kinds of salamanders. Among the 34 types of trees are the pungent Norway spruce as well as red spruce; striped, sugar, and red maples; four types of pines; and yellow poplar, sycamore, sassafras, cucumber magnolia, basswood, and elm. Azaleas, mountain laurels, rhododendrons, and spicebushes dot the mountainsides and valleys. More than 70 bird species canvass the forest: the white-breasted nuthatch, yellow-breasted chat, grosbeak, ruffed grouse, least flycatcher, raven, scarlet tanager, and 8 kinds of warblers.

MONONGAHELA: DEEP GORGE TO GREAT HEIGHTS

Returning to the Monongahela National Forest, our next stop is **Spruce Knob/Seneca Rocks National Recreation Area❖,** and more specifically its **Smoke Hole❖** unit five miles off Route 220 south of Petersburg and Landes. One explanation for the name Smoke Hole involves the mists that rise above the deep gorge cut by the South Branch of the Potomac River and waft around North Fork Mountain and Cave Mountain. Other explanations claim that ancient Native Americans smoked meats in the various caves and that early settlers made moonshine in them. The name Smoke Hole also designates other features in the area, including a commercialized cave that claims to have the world's largest ribbon stalactite and a room with a ceiling 274 feet high. The Smoke Hole unit of the national recreation area, in Pendleton and Grant counties, is one of the most scenic and ecologically interesting in the state, and the West Virginia Nature Conservancy gives it top priority for protection.

Smoke Hole has outcroppings of sandstone and limestone similar to those seen throughout the region, but its location in the rain shadow means it gets less precipitation than nearby areas, although enough rain falls to produce flash floods. Conditions have fostered cedar glades—which the Nature Conservancy reports is the only plant community found solely in West Virginia—limestone barrens, shale barrens, and stands of red pine and dwarf pine. Smoke Hole is home to peregrine falcons and bald eagles as well as colonies of the endangered Virginia big-eared bat.

The U.S. Forest Service maintains the 24-mile North Fork Mountain Trail, 3.5-mile South Branch Trail, and 1-mile Big Bend Loop Trail. Passing along a ridgetop with sweeping views of the river valley below and the distant mountains to the west, the North Fork provides a splendid vantage point for observing soaring raptors. Smoke Hole offers adventurous hikers—preferably those equipped with compass and map—plenty of opportunities to explore vast forests untouched by blazed trails. White-water canoeing is another way to enjoy nature here. Paved and unpaved roads wind in nine miles off Route 220 to the Big Bend camping area and pass spectacular Eagle Rock, a rugged outcropping named for William Eagle, a soldier in the American Revolution.

The craggiest and severest cliffs thrusting from the green mountainsides of West Virginia, Kentucky, and Tennessee are part of the formation known as **Seneca Rocks,** located at a community of the same name where Route 33 meets Route 28/55. From various viewpoints, these rock cliffs impress travelers with their massiveness or their apparent razor-sharpness, with their height or their sheerness. "Like the backbone of a gigantic prehistoric dinosaur," in naturalist Norma Jean Venable's words, Seneca Rocks looms 960 feet above North Fork Valley. The cliffs are composed of erosion-resistant Tuscarora sandstone that dates back 425 million years. Originating as eroded sediments and sands from ancient mountains, they were compressed under the weight of overlying sediments for millions of years, becoming a hard formation that was then tossed and upended into a series of folds, presumably as a result of the collision of continents some 250 million years ago. Over time, the layers eroded away, and the Seneca Rocks were exposed.

Legend has it that a Seneca princess, Snow Bird, chose a husband from among several suitors by leading them on an arduous climb to the top. In World War II, the U.S. military trained soldiers as mountain climbers on Seneca Rocks, and serious rock climbers still flock here. Today a 1.3-mile trail with a half dozen mitigating switchbacks allows adventurers of all ages to accomplish the still strenuous climb to the summit. The rocks display various hues at different elevations but are nearly white at the top. Down below, Seneca Creek descends in a series of splendid waterfalls on its way to the North Fork of the South Branch of the Potomac River. At the U.S. Forest Service's Seneca Rocks Visitor Center, exhibits explain the geology of the area. South of Seneca Rocks, evidence of underground geology can be seen at Seneca Caverns, a commercialized cave 165 feet beneath the surface that extends for more than three miles.

Although **Spruce Knob,** at 4,861 feet, is West Virginia's highest point, it does not appear to soar dramatically because the adjacent peaks along the Spruce Mountain ridge rise higher than 4,700 feet for several miles. A Pottsville Sandstone formation, Spruce Knob is almost a natural rock garden. Whispering Spruce Path winds through the peak's loose boulders and rock slabs, which are only four or five inches thick but several feet long.

One-sided red spruce are abundant here, and their propensity for sending out long branches at ground level creates a false impression

ABOVE: *Known for its speed, the peregrine falcon preys on pigeons, shorebirds, and waterfowl.*

TOP RIGHT: *Perched on the stalk of a smooth sumac, an eastern bluebird prepares to take off for a quick ground-level feeding jaunt.*

BOTTOM RIGHT: *More often heard than seen, the yellow-breasted chat issues various croaks, whistles, squeaks, and scolds, among other sounds.*

that one is walking among some form of dwarf, piney ground cover. In fact, they are often the ends of intertwining branches from a 5- or 6-foot spruce 15 feet away. This terrain is typical of a phenomenon known as krummholz, a high forest environment of trees gnarled and stunted by the wind. Just a few feet lower, however, protection from the west wind is sufficient for spruce to assume more normal shapes and for mountain ash to thrive.

Attending the struggling spruces are several species more generally associated with New England and Canada: dwarf cornel, or bunchberry; huckleberry; blueberry; mountain holly; rose azalea; and fireweed. Ruffed grouse, yellow-rumped warblers, and robins are among the birds undaunted by Spruce Knob's rigors. Bears, too, venture to these heights.

Atop Spruce Knob is a tower affording views east toward Virginia's Shenandoah National Park 38 miles away, north to Roaring Plains 14 miles away and the Allegheny Front, and west to Spruce Knob Lake. Down below, 60 miles of trails wander through dense hardwood

45

ABOVE: *Although bucks and does herd separately most of the year, in winter white-tailed deer yard up together, subsisting on a diet of twigs.*

forests. Motorists can also drive to the top via 12 miles of winding, narrow gravel roads accessed from Route 3 south of Riverton.

West of Spruce Knob, continue with the delights of the Monongahela National Forest at **Laurel Fork North Wilderness**❖ and **Laurel Fork South Wilderness**❖. Split by Route 40 west of Osceola, these 12,000 acres along Middle Mountain were designated wilderness areas by Congress in 1983 and were allowed to return to a natural state. Forests of beech, maple, black cherry, and birch give way to open, grassy areas in the narrow headwaters of the Cheat River valley. Elevation ranges from 2,900 feet to 3,700 feet. Temperatures drop from 70 degrees to 40 degrees Fahrenheit during summer nights, and winter temperatures average around the freezing mark and can drop to minus 20.

Gaudineer Scenic Area❖ provides a striking contrast to the tortured, diminutive trees atop Spruce Knob to its southeast. Here, in an area designated a natural landmark, is a tract where old-growth red spruce grow tall and unencumbered along with yellow birch, beech, red maple, and other species. Tree trunks are up to 40 inches in diameter. Encompassing 130 acres, Gaudineer is about 20 miles from Spruce Knob, north of Route 250 near Cheat Bridge.

WEST OF THE MONONGAHELA: TREES, TREES, TREES

To the west of the national forest lie two state preserves: **Kumbrabow State Forest❖,** due west of Elkwater off Route 219, and **Holly River State Park❖,** 25 miles farther west at the town of Hacker Valley on Route 20. A wild, dense forest covering nearly 9,500 acres, Kumbrabow derives its name not, as it might seem, from an ancient Native American word but from a combination of the names of three families involved in founding the park—Kump, Brady, and Bowers. At Holly River, which embraces more than 8,000 acres, trails of varying length and severity wander amid steep hillsides to several waterfalls, sphagnum moss bogs, and spruce forests.

Continuing to zigzag southward through the Monongahela National Forest, one comes to **Seneca State Forest❖** south of Dunmore on Route 92. Established in 1924, Seneca is the oldest state forest in West Virginia, encompassing 11,684 acres tucked between the Greenbrier River and Michael Mountain. Seneca Lake is a pleasant fishing spot surrounded by conifers and rhododendrons. Anglers may arrive to seek trout assiduously, but like other visitors they will soon discover the charm of solitude, birdsong, and shy wildlife. Winding for 23 miles through forests of hemlock, pine, oak, rhododendron, mosses, and wildflowers, trails range in difficulty from easy walks for nature study to more rigorous trips amid high-country rock outcroppings. Here there is access to the **Greenbrier River Trail❖,** which traverses 80 miles near several state parks and forests (see the end of this chapter).

In late summer cotton grass grows abundantly in the **Cranberry Glades Botanical Area❖,** giving the bogs a fluffy loveliness as afternoon breezes stir the tall sedge stems bearing white berries. The **Cranberry Mountain Visitor Center—** reached via Highland Scenic Highway

RIGHT: *Once plentiful, brook trout need cold water to flourish. Pollution from logging, farming, and housing has now reduced the habitat of this native fish.*

OVERLEAF: *In Monongahela National Forest, fluffy white cotton grass carpets a moist meadow at Cranberry Glades Botanical Area near Richwood, West Virginia.*

(Route 150), which extends 43 miles from Elk Mountain to Richwood—is well worth a stop for its interpretive exhibits and orientation information. The entrance to the Glades is just west of the visitor center, on Route 55. A half-mile boardwalk wanders through a bog forest, glades, grasslands, and shrub communities in a 3,400-foot-high bowl between mountains. Species at the Glades include sphagnum moss, carnivorous sundew, cranberry, and jack-in-the-pulpit growing among jewelweed, marsh marigold, water parsnip, and yew. Plant succession is unhindered here, so eventually the bog will shrink as the wetland forest establishes itself. Red spruce, hemlock, and yellow birch thrive, because their shallow root systems are well suited to the wet soil.

The backcountry conifer forests—with their sparse understory of pungent, carpeted floors—stretch away in a succession of meandering creeks, thick mats of mosses, and military-straight rows of trees spawned in the decay of a single fallen log. In the clearings, goldenrod bursts into view along with the bushy aster's delicate lavender.

In the 36,000-acre **Cranberry Wilderness❖** elevations range from 2,400 to 4,600 feet, and several recreation areas lie north and south of the Cranberry River. More than 50 miles are traversed by nine basic trails. The **Falls of Hills Creek Scenic Area** is the beginning of a hike to three delightful, little-known waterfalls. Animal species at Cranberry include black bear, white-tailed deer, wild turkey, snowshoe hare, eastern cottontail, mink, and bobcat.

Off Route 27 at Seebert to the southeast, a winding roadway underscores the steepness of the mountainous terrain and provides an impressive entrance into the darkening forest of **Watoga State Park❖.** The largest of the state's parks at 10,108 acres, Watoga derives its name from the Cherokee word *Watauga,* meaning "river of many islands." The river, which flows beside the park, is now called the Greenbrier. Trails wind through the woods known as Brooks Arboretum—in honor of entomologist and writer Fred E. Brooks—where 70 types of trees and shrubs grow. Particularly impressive are the stands of tall tulip trees, or yellow poplars, that mark some of the steep

---

LEFT: *Artist-naturalist Louis Agassiz Fuertes (1874–1927) painted this striking portrait of a wild turkey in 1910. A weak flyer that nevertheless roosts in trees, this native fowl feeds on acorns, nuts, and insects.*

slopes. Also growing along the trails are birch, hickory, magnolia, oak, pine, buckeye, balsam fir, cottonwood, cedar, sassafras, and sourwood. Chestnut saplings attest to the survival of at least the root systems of the majestic tree once prevalent in the southern Appalachians. Park rangers conduct eventide excursions to watch beavers at work.

EXITING THE MONONGAHELA

Along the border with Virginia, 11 miles northeast of Neola on Route 14, is the largest lake in the Monongahela, 165-acre Lake Sherwood, focal point of **Lake Sherwood Recreation Area❖,** which contains several trails. Beavers and ducks are often spotted from one trail that loops around the lake, and another wanders among pines, rhododendrons, and hardwoods, providing exceptional views of Meadow Creek Valley. The Connector leads to the Meadow Creek headwaters in a basin of old hardwoods, and the 300-mile Allegheny Trail also passes near the recreation area.

The 107-acre **Beartown State Park❖,** which lies between the "claws" of the Monongahela's southern end, features a boardwalk through an unusual network of rock formations and caverns shaped and pitted by heavy erosion. The eeriness of the dark, moss-covered rock formations gave rise to local legends of black bears living here. A thin layer of soil supports wildflowers amid deciduous trees, and the climate is cold enough to support some species associated more with the North. Beartown is on Route 219 about seven miles south of Hillsboro, Pearl Buck's birthplace.

Our southernmost stop in the Monongahela is **Blue Bend Recreation Area❖,** near the community of Alvon on Route 92. Although developed by the Civilian Conservation Corps in the 1930s, remote Blue Bend evokes images of a primeval forest. Three of the longer trails climb and descend through hardwood and conifer forests, ford streams, and trek beside ragwort, gentians, wild geraniums, spicebushes, rhododendrons, wild orchids, and other flowering plants. A Braille Trail provides experiences in a natural area for those who cannot use conventional trails.

There are said to be more than 1,500 caves and caverns in the region just south of the Monongahela, around Lewisburg and White Sulphur Springs. Several caves are open to the public and for the most part are highly commercialized. Fanciful tales claim that Thomas Jefferson discovered dinosaur bones at Organ Cave, named for its filigree calcite formation that resembles a cathedral pipe organ.

Kates Mountain, at 3,200 feet, is the dominant feature of **Greenbrier State Forest❖**, a 5,100-acre parcel near the resort of the same name, two miles south of Interstate 64 on Route 60 between White Sulphur Springs and Caldwell. Its typical mixed hardwood forest includes such unusual species as Kate's mountain clover and box huckleberry. A rugged ridgetop road, much of it unpaved, ascends the mountain, and near the top the roadside is sprinkled with mountain sunflowers, Jerusalem artichokes, asters, chicory, and white snakeroot. Among four trails that total nearly eight miles are Young's Nature Trail with its glades of well-spaced poplars and the more physically challenging Rocky Ridge Trail. Hart's Run Demonstration Area is designed to show how lumber production can be consistent with woodlands conservation practices.

The 77-mile **Greenbrier River Trail❖** begins north of Route 60 at Caldwell and runs north by **Beartown State Park❖, Calvin Price State Forest❖, Watoga State Park❖,** and **Seneca State Forest❖** to just south of **Cass Scenic Railroad State Park❖.** Hiking it is a great way to visit these parks and forests.

RIGHT: *West Virginia's natural areas contain a bountiful supply of native wildflowers. Displaying different shades of lavender are the rare blue fringed gentian (top) and the more common pink wild geranium (bottom).*

CHAPTER TWO

SOUTHERN AND WESTERN WEST VIRGINIA:
GOING WITH THE FLOW

Rivers dominate the landscape in southern and western West Virginia. Plenty of rivers flow in eastern West Virginia, of course, but hills and mountains demand most of the traveler's attention there. Water takes the spotlight in the rest of the state.

The major natural feature in the southern part of West Virginia is the dramatic, deep gorge carved by the New River. Geologists theorize that, despite its name, the New River is one of the oldest watercourses in North America, a remnant of the ancient Teays River that crossed the eastern half of the continent before the Ice Age.

The New River originates in North Carolina and rolls north across the Allegheny Plateau, picking up such major tributaries as the Bluestone and Greenbrier rivers and many lesser flows. After a meandering trek of 250 miles, it joins the Gauley River at the town of Gauley Bridge, and the two then form the Kanawha, which flows northwestward to join the Ohio River at Point Pleasant. The Ohio merges with the Mississippi in western Kentucky, which means that the waters of the New and its many tributaries flow into the Atlantic via the Gulf of Mexico. It is all very similar to the children's song about how the various bones of the body are connected to one another.

The New River Gorge averages 1,000 feet in depth and is cut so

---

LEFT: *Below the lacy cascades of Sandstone Falls, the bright yellow foliage of marsh purslane brightens the rock ledges of the New River Gorge. Nearby are excellent places to observe wintering waterfowl.*

55

nearly vertical along most of its route that the floodplain is only a few feet wider than the river itself. It is no wonder that this part of West Virginia remained virtually inaccessible until the Chesapeake & Ohio Railroad opened a route along the Greenbrier, New, and Kanawha rivers in 1873 to link Virginia ports with the Ohio River. In some places the gorge is so narrow that the railroad tracks are the main street of some hamlets, and some towns have a row of houses on one side of the river and another row on the other. John Henry, the legendary steel-driving man, died after winning a contest with a steam-driven drill at a C&O tunnel construction site near Hinton. A statue memorializing him stands ten miles east of Hinton on Route 3.

In 1978, Congress designated New River Gorge National River as part of the National Park System to protect 53 miles of the free-flowing stream. Ten years later another 31 miles of the Gauley and Meadow rivers were set aside as the Gauley River National Recreation Area, and 11 additional river miles became the Bluestone National Scenic River. With numerous state parks and forests, these enclaves preserve a corridor of natural and scenic areas in the central part of the state that complements the Monongahela National Forest to the east—although without its massive acreage.

Encompassing more than 62,000 acres with elevations ranging from 900 to 3,200 feet, the national river's lands embrace a wide range of habitats—ridgetops, mixed hardwood, tributary streams, floodplains, aquatic, and altered—that are found throughout the south-central part of the state and to a lesser degree in the western regions as well. Along the way, adventurers would add, the New, the Gauley, and other rivers form a revered habitat for white-water rafters as well.

Because the New River flows north, and several others flow north or west or somewhere in-between, this chapter goes with the flow, starting near Bluefield on West Virginia's southern border and heading north to Hawks Nest State Park. Then, straying back to the east a bit, it takes in some sites west of the Monongahela and goes on to the northern Panhandle, south to Charleston, and west to the Huntington area. The distances between sites in the north-central and western parts of the state are greater than elsewhere, so travelers might want to use the interstate highways more often. The best course may well be to take the paths of least resistance, just as the rivers always do.

Newell
TOMLINSON RUN STATE PARK
New Manchester

PENNSYLVANIA

Fairmont
VALLEY FALLS SP
Tygart Valley River
Grafton

OHIO

OHIO RIVER ISLANDS NAT WILDLIFE REFUGE
Parkersburg

Hughes R.

Tygart Lake
TYGART LAKE STATE PARK

NORTH BEND STATE PARK
N Fork
Cairo

ADURA SP
Belington
Buckhannon

Glenville

CEDAR CREEK STATE PARK

WEST VIRGINIA STATE WILDLIFE CENTER

Middle Fk R.

Kanawha River

Summersville Lake

Huntington

CHARLESTON

GAULEY RIVER NAT REC AREA
Gauley Bridge
Mount Nebo

Lavalette
BEECH FORK STATE PARK

KANAWHA STATE FOREST
Hernshaw

Ansted
NEW RIVER GORGE BRIDGE
HAWKS NEST SP
Lansing
BABCOCK SP

Guyandotte R.

Dunlow
CABWAYLINGO STATE FOREST

Fayetteville

CHIEF LOGAN STATE PARK
Logan

NEW RIVER GORGE NAT RIVER
Terry
Prince
Thurmond
Quinnimont Rapids

KENTUCKY

Beckley

TWIN FALLS STATE PARK
Hinton

Panther
Iaeger
Mullens
BLUESTONE NATIONAL SCENIC RIVER
BLUESTONE SP
Bluestone Lake
PIPESTEM SP

PANTHER STATE FOREST
Flattop Mtn
Bluestone River

Bramwell
PINNACLE ROCK SP
Bluefield

VIRGINIA

NORTHWEST OF BLUEFIELD: PINNACLES, PANTHERS, AND TWINS

Before heading for the rivers, take Route 52 west of Bluefield; about 10 miles west, before Bramwell, the highway passes within a few feet of a feature towering above the road that impressively illustrates millions of years of erosion. Here, in **Pinnacle Rock State Park❖,** a plaque at the entrance colorfully tells the story: "Erosion, nature's cutting tool, has

chiseled away the stone on this spur of Flattop Mountain, leaving this giant cockscomb." A hard capstone protected the craggy sandstone pillar as softer layers were eroded, leaving 56 discernible strata. On the opposite side of the entrance a similar but less imposing pillar accompanies it. Rock climbing is not allowed, but be prepared for some rugged hiking within the park's 300 acres.

There are probably no mountain lions in West Virginia today, but legends about panthers still abound in place-names and folklore. A tale about a hunter who battled a panther with his bare hands when his rifle failed gave rise to a small town and creek both named Panther about 30 miles west of Pinnacle Rock. South of the town, about eight miles from Iaeger off Route 80, the legend also lives on in **Panther State Forest❖.** The lush, wild woodland of 7,800 acres generates a sense of remoteness in the hilly coal country near the Kentucky border. The names of creeks bespeak the wild: Crane, Fox, Cub, and of course the obligatory Panther.

After a hot summer afternoon rain, steam rises off the shiny, slick rhododendrons and moist, frilly ferns. Drift Branch

ABOVE: *A wet rock ledge shelters a red and yellow wild columbine, with its delicate bell-like flowers, at Panther State Forest.*

RIGHT: *As the trees begin to bud, early spring sunlight warms the upper reaches of Pinnacle Rock in southern West Virginia.*

OVERLEAF: *Complemented by darker evergreens, hardwoods leaf out in shades of light green, patterning the slopes of Panther State Forest.*

58

LEFT: *The native eastern redbud's distinctive pink splash tells one and all that spring has arrived in West Virginia.*
RIGHT: *Its white-tipped tail blending with the snow, a red fox waits patiently to pounce on prey. In heavy snows, the tail may totally erase the fox's tracks.*

Nature Trail wanders into the denseness, which is edged by enough sunlight to allow joe-pye weed, Jerusalem artichoke, and cardinal flower to border the forest. Inside, poplar, spruce, and oak rise and twist in their usual varying postures, dictated by their youthful stretchings for sunlight. Old logs decay at their feet, nurturing new communities of smaller species. Down a hillside toward the creek, recently fallen trees seem to connect like the skeletal hands of some prehistoric giant. Sadly, the area around Panther shows signs of the declining coal economy and is laced with images of depressed rural America. But Panther's deep and lustrous greenery preserves the region's natural dignity and beauty for all.

While a late summer day's visit to **Twin Falls State Park❖** is likely to yield sightings of deer idly grazing in the sweet grass of a golf course fairway, the key attractions here are hiking trails that clamber over green mountainsides interspersed with rocky ridges, ravines, and waterfalls. The park takes its name from two rocky waterfalls—Cabin Creek Falls and Black Fork Falls on Marsh Fork—that cascade down into forest ravines and can be reached by two of the nine trails that cover 20 miles in all. Cliffside Trail rambles over fields and through woodlands to Buzzard Cliffs and Canada Cliffs. The woods are predominantly mixed oak-hickory, with abundant hemlock and rhododendron. Besides deer, shier species such as wild turkey and fox roam the 3,776-acre park. Twin Falls is on Route 97 off Route 54 north of Mullens, about 40 miles northwest of Bluefield.

THE BLUESTONE RIVER:
PATHS OF LEAST RESISTANCE

In this part of West Virginia early settlers—and possibly Native Americans before them—made stems for clay and corncob pipes out

63

of the shrub *Spiraea alba,* which has woody branches with tiny hollow centers. The shrub grows six to eight feet tall and has small fragrant white flowers that bloom throughout the summer. In some places this shrub's common name is meadowsweet, but here it is called pipestem, and a town and park—**Pipestem State Park❖,** about 25 miles northeast of Bluefield—have adopted the name.

The Bluestone River flows through a 1,200-foot gorge in the park, which is accessible via Route 20. The park is open year-round, although service on the tramway down to the river and to one of the lodges stops in late autumn. Canyon Rim Trail drops 500 feet from the plateau to a large sandstone outcropping known as Heritage Point, which offers views of the gorge. River Trail is more demanding, requiring hikers to wade across the river before heading two miles up to Pilot Ridge. A steep, paved trail leads to an observation tower atop the 3,000-foot Pipestem Knob for sweeping views of Bluestone Lake and scattered farms that appear through the bluish haze hanging over verdant mountains and valleys.

In September the park is a good place to see hawks and other migrating raptors. The 161 bird species spotted here include tundra swan, Bonaparte's gull, horned lark, American wigeon, black-bellied plover,

Above: *The belted kingfisher (top) and great blue heron (right) fish the Bluestone and other rivers in south-central West Virginia. The kingfisher often dives from a tree, while the heron stalks shallow waters.*

Left: *At Pipestem State Park, a flowering dogwood shows its scarlet fall foliage. Anthracnose, a nonnative fungus, has killed thousands of eastern dogwoods.*

American pipit (also called water pipit), and 24 types of warblers. The birds are easier to see than the 19 types of salamanders found in the park.

A seven-mile trail along the river connects Pipestem State Park with **Bluestone State Park❖.** Most of this rugged, unspoiled part of the gorge is protected within the 11-mile **Bluestone National Scenic River❖,** which has been administered by the National Park Service since 1988, when it became the state's first entry in the U.S. Wild and Scenic Rivers System. The Bluestone River runs for 77 miles from its headwaters on East River Mountain in Virginia before it joins the New River south of Hinton. About 2 miles north of that confluence the flood-control Bluestone Dam impounds the Bluestone for 2.5 miles and the New for 12 miles to create the 2,000-acre Bluestone Lake amid rounded mountain peaks and undulating valleys in the state park and Bluestone Wildlife Management Area.

Kingfishers and great blue herons are among the bird species that favor the park's warm-water stream environment. Bobcat, deer,

Overleaf: *The spectacular New River Gorge is surrounded by countless tributaries that offer their own special, low-key attractions, such as an unexpected view of a trickling waterfall touched by golden sunlight.*

ABOVE: *The New River's cool, clear waters are an ideal habitat for the colorful rainbow darter (left), a member of the perch family about the size of a minnow, and smallmouth bass (right), an anglers' favorite.*

foxes, and flocks of wild turkey are also likely to be seen roaming the 2,100-acre park. Trails wind past the lake, streams, seasonal waterfalls, and along ridgelines; the two-mile Boundary Trail leads to a cave in the forest. Just north of the dam at Belle Point, another major tributary, the Greenbrier River, joins the New. As the merging waters slow and pool, the dropping sediment creates islands and sandbars and an aquatic habitat quite different from that of the fast-flowing New farther downstream.

THE NEW RIVER: OLDEST OF ALL

For 53 miles, from Hinton northwest to Fayetteville, **New River Gorge National River❖** protects the free-flowing river, offering some of the best white-water rafting in the East. The river and floodplain narrow as they move northward and the rapids generally become more severe. Whether on foot or in a canoe or raft, the New invites exploration, although those on the water between Thurmond and Fayetteville may be too preoccupied with the rapids to admire the scenery. The park includes a number of historic sites primarily related to coal mining, and park rangers interpret the area's natural and cultural resources at various locations. This area was also heavily logged, but second-growth forests have restored or are quickly restoring the landscape.

Off Route 20 just before Hinton, River Road heads north on the western side of the New toward one of the most enticing wonders of

ABOVE: *Measuring just a few inches long with ten thoracic legs, crayfish resemble miniature lobsters but dwell only in freshwater and never in the tropics. They are prey for a variety of fish, birds, and mammals.*

the gorge, **Sandstone Falls.** Created by a sturdy rim of Stony Gap sandstone, the creamy, churning falls are 10 to 25 feet deep and cascade over a distance of 1,200 feet. Several rare plant species grow here, including scouring rush, mud plantain, purple cliffbreak, dwarf dandelion, rockspike moss, and the Kentucky coffee tree.

The deepest section of the gorge in the national river's route can be accessed via Interstate 64 east of Beckley at **Grandview,** a former state park that has been added to the national river. From here, the view of the 1,440-foot gorge and one of the river's great oxbows, Horseshoe Bend, is grand indeed. When seen from Grandview (or from the eastern side of the river at Quinnimont, Prince, or Terry) the chasm presents what seems to be a single span of greenery, but due to variations in altitude and moisture there are actually several flora and fauna communities here.

Because the lands bordering the river are subject to periodic flooding, different species—willows, sycamores, birches, silver maples, catalpas, and honey locusts—thrive at different locations, depending upon local soils and other variations. Lovely wildflowers such as touch-me-not, buttonbush, spiderwort, trumpet creeper, and horse nettle blossom along the river's banks, and beaver and the southern flying squirrel flourish here. The water itself is home to catfish, bigmouth chub, rainbow darter, crayfish, smallmouth bass, rock bass, and a half-dozen types of mussels. Maple, poplar, oak, and hemlock thrive farther up the hillsides, along

LEFT: *A male wood duck, with its iridescent red and green head and stippled burgundy chest, surveys a wetland from a tree. Wood ducks commonly roost in tree cavities as much as 50 feet above the ground or in elevated nest boxes.*

RIGHT: *One of the most abundant birds in the eastern deciduous woodlands, a red-eyed vireo takes a break from its dawn-to-dusk singing to tend its voracious young in their suspended, cuplike nest.*

FAR RIGHT: *Often found in oak forests or along willow-lined streams, the adult male summer tanager sports a bright red coat similar to the cardinal's but has a yellow instead of a red bill.*

well-drained slopes. Evergreens, oaks, and hickories share the ridgetops, and rhododendrons, especially in their glorious burst of spring bloom, become the most conspicuous understory plant in the gorge. About 40 bird species are sighted routinely. Overhead flit bright black-and-yellow hooded warblers, summer tanagers, red-eyed vireos, and peregrine falcons, while great blue herons, wood ducks, and buffleheads ply the river's currents.

Another overlook of the New River is presented on the eastern side at **Babcock State Park**❖ off Route 41. About half of Babcock's more than 4,000 acres are wild and undeveloped, and the more than 20 miles of trails provide views of Manns Creek and Glade Creek, tributaries of the New. Babcock puts on a fine wildflower display from late spring through early summer, especially in June, when two types of rhododendrons bloom—first, the purple *catawbiense,* and then the white *maximum,* which is the state flower.

The national river's **Canyon Rim Visitor Center,** on Route 19 west of Fayetteville near Lansing, has exhibits and numerous publications about the area's natural and human history, as well as a wonderful view of the 3,030-foot-long New River Gorge Bridge. With an arch that measures 1,700 feet, this is the largest single-arch steel span

bridge in the world, and at 876 feet above the river it is the second highest bridge in the United States. On Bridge Day, the second Saturday of October, it is open to pedestrians, and parachuting and rappelling are allowed. At Canyon Rim or Grandview information is available about the area's more than 25 trails to waterfalls, geological formations, scenic sights, and old coal and railroad towns.

Just north of the national river area, on Route 60 west of Ansted, is **Hawks Nest State Park❖,** named for the hawks that soar at great heights here. Although a dam has tamed and turned the river into a large lake here, Hawks Nest's 276 acres border a dramatically rugged section of the New River Gorge. A small museum displays artifacts of Native Americans and early European settlers.

About 20 miles to the northeast, off Route 19 west of Mount Nebo, is **Summersville Lake,** the major jumping-off place for white-water enthusiasts using the **Gauley River National Recreation Area❖.** Regular water releases from Summersville Dam in September and October make the Gauley west of the dam one of the most adventurous white-water boating places in the East. The names of the class V rapids attest to their rigors and dangers: Lost Paddle, Upper and Lower Mash, Heaven Help You, and Pure Screaming Hell. Keep your eyes open and try to take in

71

the splendid natural scene as you barrel through. Six miles of the Meadow River, which flows into the Gauley from the south, also are protected within the recreation area and offer more relaxed nature studies.

At the town of Gauley Bridge, the New and Gauley rivers merge to form the Kanawha, and nearby, along Route 39, is **Cathedral Falls.** Merely a trickle in dry times, the falls then reveals its network of diagonal and horizontal rock strata in shapes suggestive of a cubist canvas by Braque or Picasso. On the other side of Gauley Bridge is **Kanawha Falls,** a picturesque series of cascades that span the breadth of the Kanawha River.

ON THE PLATEAU: A HOP, SKIP, AND JUMP

From this point on, the itinerary takes a hop toward the northeast, a skip to the northern Panhandle, and a jump south and west to the Charleston and Huntington areas on the Allegheny Plateau.

Well to the north and east of Charleston, 25 miles west of Interstate 79 and 5 miles south of Glenville on Route 33, is **Cedar Creek State Park❖.** The creek meanders through the park's 2,400 acres of rolling hills and flat valleys, which attract grouse, quail, chipmunks, deer, and groundhogs. Some of the ten miles of trails follow abandoned logging roads and animal paths through the predominant oaks and poplars.

A hint of nature, albeit in a structured environment, distinguishes the **West Virginia State Wildlife Center❖,** 12 miles south of Buckhannon, about 40 miles northeast of Cedar Creek. The center is on Route 20. The 300 acres of meadows and woods allow visitors to learn about and watch animals in a setting more nearly approximating a native habitat than most zoos. Bears, elk, bison, wolves, eagles, coyotes, wild boars, mountain lions, and river otters can be seen.

Just off Route 250 northwest of Belington, about a 20-mile drive from Buckhannon, is **Audra State Park❖,** best known for its rocky beach, which stretches beside the glistening, invitingly green Middle Fork River. In the spring, because of snowmelt and rain, the river thunders through, and thereby gives the 355-acre park its name, Audra, the Lithuanian word for thunderstorm. Only three miles of trails traverse the park, one of which leads to a cave tucked among hardwoods and conifers.

Created after the U.S. Army Corps of Engineers built Grafton Dam in 1938, **Tygart Lake State Park❖,** completed in 1947, became a popular boating and fishing center. For more than six miles five trails weave through forests resplendent with sycamore, oak, birch, and beech. The 2,134-acre park is off Route 119 south of Grafton, about 20 miles north of Belington.

North of Tygart Lake and ten miles south of Fairmont, within

ABOVE: *With a fold of skin that acts like a sail, the southern flying squirrel glides up to 240 feet, maneuvering from treetop to the ground. Nocturnal, it feeds on a variety of nuts, seeds, and berries.*
LEFT: *The white-spotted reddish-brown coats of young deer help protect them. Here a fawn is nearly camouflaged in a spring meadow of white clover, oxeye daisies, and yellow hawksweed.*
OVERLEAF: *An attractive pond grass called water-willow provides a bright yellow autumnal border for a quiet lake at Tomlinson Run State Park in the Panhandle.*

Valley Falls State Park❖, the Tygart River rushes across stony ledges, creating lacy waterfalls of 12 and 18 feet. Known as Evil Spirit Falls to the Cherokee, the cascades today are a wonderful introduction to two miles of canyon.

NORTHERN PANHANDLE AND THE OHIO

More than 100 miles north in the peak of the northern Panhandle the traveler finds **Tomlinson Run State Park❖,** three miles off Route 2 between New Manchester and Newell, about 30 miles northwest of Pittsburgh. At altitudes that range from 700 to 1,200 feet, Tomlinson Run has carved a steep gorge that drops approximately 100 feet per mile as the stream rushes toward its confluence with the Ohio River just a mile to the west of this 1,400-acre park's border. Much of the park has been designated as wilderness. Shale and sandstone cliffs tower above the narrow Beech Trail, one of a half-dozen that wander through forests of hickory, wild cherry, maple, birch, hemlock, and ash, where rhododendron, mayflower, wild hydrangea, various ferns, and American yew populate the understory. A 29-acre lake attracts some 100 species of birds.

Left: *Along the Guyandotte Beauty Trail at Chief Logan State Park, the bracts of white dogwood in bloom seem to float effortlessly between the forest floor and canopy.*
Right: *Delicate spring-blooming Virginia bluebells brighten the brown decaying leaves on the forest floor at Chief Logan.*

The temptation to feed white-tailed deer apparently accustomed to meals on wheels should be resisted at **North Bend State Park❖,** more than 90 miles back south. The park is 17 miles east of Parkersburg off Route 31S, about 8 miles northeast of Cairo, where the North Fork of the Hughes River makes a graceful horseshoe bend. Because access is difficult, some areas along the North Fork River escaped logging in earlier times, so today huge specimens of sycamore, hemlock, oak, pine, and poplar are visible to hikers. Steep and arduous, some of the nine trails pass numerous outcroppings and boulders; the self-guided Extra Mile Trail provides natural-history interpretation for the disabled and has signs in braille. The **North Bend Rail Trail❖** also runs through the park. Open to hikers, bikers, and horseback riders, this trail goes through 12 old railroad tunnels and over 32 bridges in the 61 miles between Wolf Summit in Harrison County and Walker in Wood County.

Among the most intriguing natural areas of West Virginia are the 38 islands that dot the **Ohio River** as it marks the state's northwestern boundary for nearly 360 miles. Native Americans camped on these remote islands, and in the eighteenth century George Washington reportedly surveyed some of them. Today the islands—most accessible only by boat—and their surrounding waters are rich habitats and sanctuaries for more than 50 fish species, including the endangered pink mucket pearly mussel, wood ducks and other avians, deer, beaver, mink, and dozens of rare plants. Even though they have long attracted the attention of humans, some of the islands still have virgin stands of sycamores and silver maples.

Eighteen islands are protected as the **Ohio River Islands National Wildlife Refuge❖,** which has an office in Parkersburg. **Blennerhassett Island**—where Harman Blennerhassett established a grand home in 1798 and supposedly plotted with Aaron Burr in 1806 to establish an empire in the Southwest—is now a state historical park featuring a nature preserve as well as the reconstructed mansion. The island is served by a ferry docked near 2nd and Juliana streets in Parkersburg, where the **Blennerhassett Museum** features items owned by the family and an archaeological exhibit.

CHARLESTON AND WEST

Just six miles southwest of Interstate 77 and the state capital of Charleston, **Kanawha State Forest❖** is one of West Virginia's most utilized natural areas, boasting more than 1,000 species of trees and plants, including 23 types of wild orchids, within its 9,474 acres. Seven types of sunflowers, for instance, were in bloom there in the late summer of 1994. Fourteen trails wind for 25 miles amid various forest communities, and their names evoke their history or portend their attributes: Wildcat Ridge, Rocky Ridge, Pigeon Roost, Mossy Rock, and Hemlock Falls. They provide glimpses of the rich vegetation, including the fleshy little touch-me-nots, the sinewy American hornbeam, hemlocks, papaws, umbrella magnolias, witch hazels, asters, cardinal flowers, joe-pye weed, bloodroot, sycamores, sassafras, and a wealth of goldenrod. Kanawha also has an excellent paved interpretative trail, the Spotted Salamander, for users of wheelchairs.

In the spring wildflower hikes at **Chief Logan State Park❖** are likely to provide a visual and olfactory study of columbine, buttercups, lance-leaved coreopsis, various asters, vervains, lobelia, and the rare Guyandotte beauty (the Guyandotte River flows nearby). One trail wanders through abandoned coal mines and equipment. The forest trails tend to be steep at this 3,303-acre preserve, which is 40 miles south of Charleston, off Route 119 about two miles north of the town of Logan. The park and town were named for an eloquent Mingo chief

---

LEFT: *Kanawha State Forest boasts 23 different kinds of wild orchids, including (clockwise from top left) the acid-loving rosebud; the rose-crested, a wetland inhabitant; the yellow fringed, which grows in meadows and open woods; and the wonderfully fragrant showy orchis.*

LEFT: *In Chief Logan, the still life of a lush New York fern in front of a thriving blue cohosh belies the park's location in the heart of West Virginia's coalfields.*

RIGHT: *Near the Kentucky border, the setting sun highlights the lichen-covered tree trunks of red oak and white oak and creates a shimmering carpet of moss at Cabwaylingo State Forest.*

who was appointed secretary to William Penn and then defeated at the Battle of Point Pleasant in 1774.

About 25 miles west of Logan **Cabwaylingo State Forest❖** sprawls over 8,123 acres off Route 152, about three miles southeast of Dunlow. The forest gets its name from a combination of the counties it serves—Cabell, Wayne, Lincoln, and Mingo. Elevations range from 740 to 1,250 feet, not seemingly dramatic, but 35 percent of the slopes have a grade of 40 degrees or more. An exhilarating trek is to climb the 76 stone steps to Spruce Creek Picnic Area and then make your way along the ridge trail. Various trails pass through hardwood forests laced with hemlocks, handsome umbrella magnolias, and wildflowers, including the rare crested dwarf iris. Numerous little streams feed into Twelvepole Creek.

A history of flooding plagued the area that was turned into **Beech Fork State Park❖** off routes 152 and 52 about 12 miles south of Huntington in the western corner of the state. The U.S. Army Corps of Engineers built a dam at Lavalette and, starting in 1977, backed up the two forks of Twelvepole Creek to create a 720-acre lake, which now covers an area where periodic floods had disrupted the lives of 400 families for generations. Six miles of trails wander through forests and over ridges in this 3,981-acre park. Ferns found at Beech Fork include Christmas, rattlesnake, sensitive, maidenhair, ebony spleenwort, and bracken. The staghorn sumac tree is common here and throughout West Virginia and the neighboring states of Kentucky and Tennessee. But the three states have a lot more in common than sumac, as the tours in subsequent chapters make clear.

KENTUCKY

PART TWO

K E N T U C K Y

Kentucky, like West Virginia, is a child of Virginia although it left home 71 years earlier than its sibling, in 1792, to become the 15th state. Long and narrow, like Tennessee to the south, Kentucky extends about 425 miles from east to west. From its irregular northern boundary, it measures at most 180 miles north to south narrowing to about 40 miles in the west. With 40,395 square miles, the state ranks 37th in area, just behind its mother.

The eastern part of Kentucky sits on a piece of the Cumberland Plateau, a greatly eroded mountainous area of peaks, natural arches, and bluffs that are a feast for the eye and spirit. Its north Cumberland Mountains elevations average 1,300 feet, and at Black Mountain in the southeastern corner next to Virginia they rise to a state record of 4,145 feet.

North-central Kentucky is what springs to mind when most people think of Kentucky: the state's signature, the Bluegrass region of fenced horse farms and rolling green hills enriched by the underlying layers of limestone. Bordering the Bluegrass to the south are The Knobs, a narrow belt of conical hills, and the Pennyroyal, or Pennyrile, a region similar to the Bluegrass on the surface but underlain with younger limestone formations that have eroded into hundreds of caverns, including the world's longest, Mammoth Cave.

Traveling west, the lands gradually become less rugged and lower in elevation. Along the Mississippi River are marshes, swamps, and bottomland forests in the Gulf Coastal Plain. The lowest point is 257 feet in Fulton County at the southwestern extreme of the state.

Kentucky is nearly surrounded by rivers. At Kentucky's northernmost point the Ohio River marks the approximate southern terminus of the great Ice Age glaciers. Flowing west from West Virginia, the Ohio also forms Kentucky's northern border with Ohio, Indiana, and Illinois before it merges with the Mississippi north of Wickliffe. The state shares both the

PRECEDING PAGES: *Near Lexington, spring green suffuses the tree-topped ravine and rushing waters of the Kentucky River at Raven Run. The rocks in this limestone gorge are more than 430 million years old.*

Cumberland and Tennessee rivers with its southern neighbor, but claims most of Lake Barkley, Kentucky Lake, and Land Between the Lakes for itself. The Big Sandy River and its Tug Fork tributary form the boundary with West Virginia. The Kentucky River begins near the Virginia border and flows northwest through the Bluegrass area into the Ohio.

Kentucky was a heavily forested, wildlife-rich hunting territory for the Shawnee, Chickasaw, and Cherokee. European settlers to the east heard of the wonders of the West, but only a few tried to explore the land beyond the mountains until Dr. Thomas Walker and then Daniel Boone made their way through Cumberland Gap in the mid-1700s. It was Walker who called the river Cumberland for William Augustus, the Duke of Cumberland and son of King George II. Later the name was liberally affixed to all sorts of places—the gap, the mountains, the plateau, a major waterfall, and a lake among them. The name Boone and its derivatives are equally widespread.

The thousands of pioneers who flowed into Kentucky on the Wilderness Trail may have thought this lush paradise of plants and wildlife, including great herds of buffalo, would last forever. In a relatively short time, however, most of the virgin forests were logged, and the hills were mined so extensively that the state is now the nation's largest producer of bituminous coal. The state's Fish and Wildlife Commission says that today only about 385,000 acres of wetlands remain out of an original 1,600,000 acres. Various state and private organizations—including the Nature Conservancy, Audubon Society, and Kentucky State Nature Preserves Commission—are working to protect these and other natural resources, and they've had some success: Nearly 50 percent of the timberlands have been reforested.

Despite commercial pressure Kentucky's natural features are still abundant. More than 200 bird species, including the state bird, the cardinal, are common, and another 100 are inhabitants. Most live in forests of oak, maple, birch, pine, sycamore, hickory, and the state tree, the tulip (yellow poplar). Flourishing in the understory are rhododendron, mountain laurel, and some 2,000 species of wildflowers, ferns, and weeds that embrace an array of asters, coreopsis, honeysuckle, sunflowers, violets, dragonhead, and the state flower, goldenrod. Shades of yellow, red, blue, and white add spice to the swamplands, the rolling bluegrass, and plunging gorges.

OVERLEAF: *In his 1881–82 painting* **Falls of the Cumberland River,** *Carl C. Brenner (1838–88), a Louisville sign painter now better remembered for his landscapes, captured the majesty of the state's best-known cascade.*

EASTERN KENTUCKY:
CIRCLING THE PLATEAU

These are haunted places, or at least it is easy to feel haunted in them, alone at nightfall," wrote Kentuckian Wendell Berry in his essay "An Entrance to the Woods" about a walk and overnight stay in Red River Gorge. "As the air darkens and the cool of the night rises, one feels the immanence of the wraiths of the ancient tribesmen who used to inhabit the rock houses of the cliffs; of the white hunters from east of the mountains; of the farmers who accepted the isolation of these nearly inaccessible valleys to crop the narrow bottoms and ridges and pasture their cattle and hogs in the woods; of the seekers of quick wealth in timber and ore. For though this is a wilderness place, it bears its part of the burden of human history. If one spends much time here and feels much liking for the place, it is hard to escape the sense of one's predecessors."

In these few sentences Berry conveys the essence of the Appalachian mosaic that makes up eastern Kentucky and just how much our forebears remain an integral part of the landscape. Appropriately, the tour loop begins around Kentucky's Cumberland Plateau where many early residents found a way into and through the Appalachian wilderness: at the Cumberland Gap. Travelers who get out of their cars and walk in the woodlands, canyons, and mountains at Cumberland Gap

LEFT: *Amid jagged crevices and rocky outcrops, autumn begins in bright splashes of reds and yellows at the Clinchfield Overlook in Breaks Interstate Park, which straddles Kentucky and Virginia.*

and at the other parks and reserves, like Berry, can "function at foot speeds" and renew their senses in the natural world.

From Cumberland Gap, the loop heads northeast along Pine Mountain to places with such intriguing names as Kingdom Come and Bad Branch River and goes on to the rugged, deep canyon at Breaks Interstate Park that crosses into Virginia.

Continuing north, the tour visits lakes, Carter Caves, and the countryside around Greenup, where educator-writer Jesse Stuart lived and where "the Little Sandy River runs near and the waters can be heard going over the stony riffles on silent nights. ...[where] we could hear the foxes barking from the lonely hilltops.... And snakes often writhed through the tall weeds not far from our door."

Then circling southwest the itinerary leads to the multifarious forests, gorges, arches, waterfalls, and other riches within the Daniel Boone National Forest, including state parks and Berry's Red River Gorge. The route through the national forest is indeed circuitous, but if travelers take their time and use maps, they should find the way. "I can't say I was ever lost," Daniel Boone has been quoted as saying, "but I was bewildered once for three days." Visitors will soon find that there are worse fates than being bewildered in Kentucky.

Above: *Kentucky's state bird, the showy red cardinal, is a real songster, issuing its distinctive, descending choruses of* sweet-sweet-sweet-sweet *from high, exposed perches.*
Overleaf: *Viewed from Pinnacle Overlook, touches of early fall foliage help define the Cumberland Gap, an area rich in natural and cultural history. Fern Lake is visible in the distance.*

CUMBERLAND GAP: THE WAY THROUGH

For many years the sheer presence of the southern Appalachian Mountains restricted European settlers to life along the eastern seaboard. Then in the mid-eighteenth century they discovered a way through the mountains, one that had been created by buffalo and other animals in their seasonal migrations and had long been used by Native Americans

EASTERN KENTUCKY

25   0   25 Miles
25   0   25 Kilometers

OHIO RIVER

South Portsmouth

Greenup

Greenbo Lake State Resort Park

Jesse Stuart Nature Preserve

OHIO

Tygart State For.

Carter Caves State Resort Park

Ashland

Olive Hill

WEST VIRGINIA

Morehead

Salt Lick

DANIEL BOONE

Lexington

Winchester

Mountain Pkwy

Pilot Knob SNP

Clifty Wilderness

Slade

Natural Bridge State Resort Park

Red River Gorge Geological Area

Mississippian Plateau

Russell Fk. Big Sandy R.

Prestonsburg

Jenny Wiley State Resort Park

N Fk. of the Kentucky R.

Middle Fk. of the Kentucky R.

S Fork of the Kentucky R.

NAT FOREST

McKee

Sheltowee Trace Nat Rec Trail

Red Bird R.

Mill Creek WMA

London

Cane Creek Wildlife Mgt Area

Levi Jackson State Park

Corbin

Beaver Wildlife Mgt Area

Greenwood

Cumberland Falls State Resort Park

DANIEL BOONE NF

Lilley Cornett Woods

Kingdom Come SP

Blackey

Bad Branch River SNP

Cumberland

Black Mtn

Cumberland Mtns

Elkhorn City

The Towers

BREAKS INTERSTATE PARK

Cumberland Plateau

Big Laurel

Kentenia State Forest

Harlan

Pine

VIRGINIA

Pine Mtn State Resort Park

Pineville

Kentucky Ridge State Forest

Shillalah Cr WMA

Cubage

Cranks Creek Wildlife Management Area

Middlesboro

Cumberland Gap National Historical Park

Big South Fork Nat River & Rec Area

Cumberland Gap

TENNESSEE

Licking River

Cumberland R.

LEFT: *Two bald eagles survey the landscape from a dead tree limb. Since the ban of DDT in the 1970s, the national bird has made a strong comeback and is now often seen soaring over the Cumberland Gap and other Appalachian ridges.*

for both trade and war in their travels between the Potomac and the Ohio. That place today is protected in **Cumberland Gap National Historical Park❖,** a 20,200-acre enclave shared by Kentucky, Tennessee, and Virginia. The park entrance is along Route 25E east of Middlesboro.

Dr. Thomas Walker first came upon the gap in 1750 when he was hired by the Loyal Land Company of Virginia to stake out a grant beyond the mountains. Although Walker did not find the Bluegrass area, he did find a way through the seemingly impregnable Appalachians. The passage was later used by Daniel Boone in his pioneer trips of the 1760s, and in 1775 Boone led a group of 30 men who marked the old Warriors Path through the gap into the interior. It became known as the Wilderness Trail and was followed by thousands of pioneers in their restless westward migrations. By the end of the Revolutionary War about 12,000 people had crossed into the new territory, and by 1792 the state, newly admitted to the Union, had more than 74,000 residents. The trail became a road by 1796 and remained a major route west until the early 1800s, when it was supplanted by northern canals, railroads, and the Mississippi.

Today one can stand in the park at the chain-enclosed **Pinnacle Overlook** at an elevation of 2,240 feet and see the impressive vista that greeted early explorers and settlers, walk the half-mile Wilderness

Road Trail that follows the original route through the gap, and travel the Wilderness Road itself—Route 25E to the north into Kentucky and Route 58 to the east into Virginia. But, first, it is worth spending some time here hiking the 50 miles of trails along the ridges and valleys. Nearby are such places as the **Hensley Settlement,** a former self-sustaining mountain community with log houses and split-rail fences, and **Sand Cave,** which is one of the largest rock houses (large, shallow caves) in the eastern United States. The acre-size Sand Cave is named for the deep layer of sand that accumulated over the centuries and now covers its floor. Near the cave is a 25-foot waterfall. From Pinnacle Overlook a 21-mile trail follows the ridge northeast across the length of the park, and the **Cumberland Trail❖** starts its 200-mile route south through Tennessee toward the Alabama line.

The thick forests that beckoned Walker and Boone were for the most part indiscriminately logged. In their place today stand second-growth woods of oak, hickory, and yellow poplar, interspersed with Virginia pine, maple, and hemlock. Overhead, turkey vultures, hawks, and an occasional bald eagle soar on the air waves above the mountain pass.

About 20 miles north of Cumberland Gap, off Route 987 near Cubbage, the Kentucky Department of Fish and Wildlife Resources maintains the 2,600-acre **Shillalah Creek Wildlife Management Area❖** of old-growth forests and high, rugged cliffs.

Along Pine Mountain

Near Pineville, on the Wilderness Road a few miles northwest of Cumberland Gap, is **Pine Mountain State Resort Park❖.** The park takes its name not from one peak but from a single mountain mass that is 25 miles wide and stretches 125 miles along the southwest-to-northeast alignment of the entire plateau. Elevations range from about 2,000 feet near the park entrance on Route 25E to more than 3,200 far to the northeast. Although modest in elevation, Pine Mountain provides wonderfully scenic spots, ranging from impressive cliffs to quiet cove forests. A variety of rock formations delight hikers. Geologists describe this long ridge as an overthrust block that was pushed laterally.

Nine miles of trails lead to such features as Chained Rock, where local citizens installed a massive chain that is supposed to protect Pineville from a rock slide, and Honeymoon Falls. Couples can deter-

95

LEFT: *The wild turkey, Benjamin Franklin's choice for the national bird, is regaining its range in Kentucky thanks to wildlife management programs.*
RIGHT: *Looming over the small community of Pineville in southeastern Kentucky, Chained Rock is a popular feature of Pine Mountain State Resort Park.*

mine if there is any connection between the two features and then take the Lost Trail to the former site of an old moonshine still. Spring is particularly colorful when the blossoms of redbud and rhododendron dot the hardwood forest, and the prevalent mountain laurel lends its name to an annual festival held the last weekend in May.

Within the park about 780 acres of Pine Mountain's southern slope have been designated as a nature preserve to protect the pale corydalis, a delicate pink-and-yellow flower that grows on sandstone outcroppings here and nowhere else in the state. The pale blue gentian, with its vertical stripes, is another rare plant protected here. One trail follows an old streambed studded with numerous boulders to massive hemlocks in an 86-acre old-growth forest near the park border. The state park is within the 11,363-acre **Kentucky Ridge State Forest❖,** which can be entered five miles southwest of Pineville on Route 190.

For a look at the unchained wilderness as Walker and Boone might have seen it, head east to **Cranks Creek Wildlife Management Area❖.** These 1,500 acres administered by the Kentucky Department of Fish and Wildlife Resources are 15 miles southeast of Harlan via Route 421 to Route 1138 (Stone Mountain Road). Immediately past the entrance, this rugged area, home of wild turkeys, deer, and various raptors, becomes steep and dense with vegetation. On a rainy August afternoon, with Cranks Creek roaring, the preserve provides a challenging contrast even to the relatively strenuous hiking at nearby parks. Of special interest here are Herb Smith Lake and a wagon road tunnel at the top of Stone Mountain.

The 38-mile **Little Shepherd Trail,** a narrow paved and gravel road for both hikers and motorized vehicles, winds from Harlan northeast to Whitesburg, passing through **Kentenia State Forest❖,**

where it abuts the southern tip of the Redbird Purchase Unit of Daniel Boone National Forest on Route 510 south of Big Laurel. The trail gets its name from *The Little Shepherd of Kingdom Come,* a 1903 novel of the Civil War by John Fox, Jr., set in the Cumberland Mountains; the trail, perhaps to no one's surprise, runs through **Kingdom Come State Park❖.** Here Pine Mountain and the Cumberlands as a whole take on a rounder, gentler look. From the park entrance on Route 1254, off Route 119 near the village of Cumberland, there is an unobstructed view of the highest point in Kentucky, graceful **Black Mountain** at 4,145 feet.

Sites within the park include Log Rock, an elongated sandstone arch that resembles a huge log, and Raven Rock, a stark sandstone formation that juts out of the ridgetop like an ocean liner held fast by a sea of sand. Its coloration ranges from a rich brown at its base to a sun-bleached beige at its broad top. An idyllic rhododendron thicket borders the floral Possum Trail. A portion of the park is set aside as a nature preserve to protect the state's third largest population of the Indiana myotis, also called the social myotis, an endangered bat species. Line Fork Cave serves as a winter roost for more than 3,000 of the animals, about 30 percent of the total that formerly lived there. Because of the decrease, access to the cave is by permit only, from May through August.

A gem tucked away north of Kingdom Come, **Lilley Cornett Woods**❖ is a small cove forest that has escaped the ravages of logging, mining, and building over the years, although a dispute has flared anew over whether underground coal mining would damage the ecology above. Lilley Cornett, who refused to allow any cutting except of afflicted

chestnut trees, bought the land after World War I, and it remained in his family until 1969, when it was purchased by the state. Now supporting about 90 species of trees and shrubs and 500 types of flowering plants, Cornett Woods serves as the Appalachian Ecological Research Station of Eastern Kentucky University. Of the 554 acres, 252 acres are virgin forest with coves, steep slopes, benches, and ridges. This old-growth woodland is described as mixed mesophytic, a forest with several species vying for dominance, in this case sugar maple, white oak, American beech, basswood, and yellow poplar. Wehrle's salamander, one of Kentucky's rarest wildlife species, lives at Cornett Woods. Southwest of Blackey on Route 1103, the preserve is open to visitors only via guided tours, which are offered daily from May 15 through August 15, on spring and fall weekends, and other times by appointment.

ABOVE: *Lilley Cornett Woods is home to Wehrle's salamander, rare in Kentucky. Dwelling in rocky crevices or under rocks or logs, it feeds on spiders and centipedes.*

LEFT: *A white bank of low, fluffy clouds rolls in against Pine Mountain in the Cumberlands, reinforcing the site's heavenly name: Kingdom Come State Park.*

OVERLEAF: *As it cuts through Pine Mountain, the Russell Fork of the Big Sandy River reflects The Towers, a major geologic formation at Breaks Interstate Park.*

Nearby, to the west on Pine Mountain, **Bad Branch State Nature Preserve**❖ protects more species than any other area in the state. Plants growing here include Fraser's sedge and Michaux's saxifrage, both named for early botanists who explored the Appalachians, plus

ABOVE: *The fragrant yellow lady's slipper grows in limestone wetlands.*
LEFT: *The pink lady's slipper prefers dry forests, especially pine woods.*

matricary grapefern, painted trillium, and rose pogonia. The preserve protects such rare fish and mammals as the arrow darter; long-tailed, masked, and pygmy shrews; and the woodland jumping mouse. A pair of common ravens also nest here. The scenery is good, too, as Bad Branch tumbles down 1,000 feet of the mountain's south face in less than three miles, deeply eroding the slope and plunging in a 60-foot waterfall into a gorge marked by high sandstone cliffs and boulders. The entrance is on Route 932 off Route 119.

Breaks Interstate Park❖ occupies the northeastern end of Pine Mountain. Here rugged crevices are slashed from below and ornate rock formations garnish the deep canyons. The most spectacular vista is of The Towers, an immense knob created by the Russell Fork of the Big Sandy River. Reminiscent of a Bavarian fortress in a fairy tale, The Towers borders a horseshoe bend where the river cuts, or breaks, a five-mile, 1,000-foot-deep canyon through Pine Mountain—

one of the deepest canyons east of the Mississippi. After the water slowly wore through the mountain's sandstone layers, it cut through the softer shale quickly (in geologic time) and nearly vertically.

The park is named for the break in the elongated mountain and because it straddles the border of Kentucky and Virginia, where most of its 4,600 acres lie. It is reached from Kentucky via Route 80 about eight miles southeast of Elkhorn City. More than ten miles of trails provide numerous glimpses of great walls of rock, natural bridges, dense forests, and the boulder-strewn Russell Fork, a white-water rafting area. Overlook Trail winds along exposed rock high above the canyon. For less adventuresome souls, a nature drive of less than a mile provides a close look at a section of the forest. Some of the more than 60 species of trees are identified along Chestnut Ridge Trail and Geological Trail. Species include yellow poplar, various oaks, beech, black walnut, witch hazel, hemlock, sweet birch, sourwood, box elder, and American holly. Wildflowers abound: Dutchman's-breeches, yellow and pink lady's slippers, arrow-leaved violets, bluebells, flame azaleas, and several types of trilliums and rhododendrons.

DEWEY LAKE TO CARTER CAVES:
TRAILS, LAKES, AND CAVES

Jenny Wiley State Resort Park❖, three miles east of Prestonsburg on Route 3 off Route 23/460, is highly developed, with a scenic chairlift, marina, and amphitheater. It is also the southern end of the 163-mile **Jenny Wiley National Recreation Trail❖,** which commemorates the travails and triumphs of a pioneer woman who was held captive by the Shawnee, escaped, and wandered through the wilderness before eventually finding her family. (The northern end is at South Portsmouth near the Ohio River.) At nearby **Dewey Lake** the U.S. Army Corps of Engineers maintains a steep and rugged 10,000-acre wilderness area that is completely forested.

Ambling through a hollow beside Greenbo Lake west of Ashland about 50 miles to the north, hikers may well chance upon a family of white-tailed deer darting adroitly up the hill, the speckled fawn passing in and out of sight, camouflaged by the forest's pine-needle carpet. **Greenbo Lake State Resort Park❖** and nearby **Jesse Stuart State Nature Preserve** provide more than ten miles of trails, most of them over

ABOVE: *The endangered gray myotis is a true cave dweller and one of a number of bat species that are now threatened because of flooding, an increase in caving, and the commercialization of many caverns.*

moderately rugged terrain. An educator known for his books and poems about the Kentucky Appalachians, Stuart lived in W Hollow, 730 acres of which is now protected by the preserve and open to the public, although his house is private. The park lodge displays Stuart memorabilia. Take Fern Valley Trail to see club moss along with live Christmas ferns and shade-tolerant redbuds and dogwoods under a high canopy of pines. The 7-mile Michael Tygart Loop visits old home-steads and should not be confused with the 24-mile Michael Tygart Trail that links up with the 180-mile Jenny Wiley National Recreation Trail. The park is off Route 1 about 14 miles north of Interstate 64, and the preserve is 5 miles farther north toward Greenup. Both are natural delights in an area that has seen its share of industry.

The elaborate chemistry of living limestone caves is exemplified at **Carter Caves State Resort Park❖,** off Interstate 64 at Olive Hill, about 10 miles south and 10 miles west of Greenbo. Located in a narrow sliv-er of the Mississippian Plateau that extends here from its cave-country core in the central-western part of the state, the park has several natural bridges and tunnels and more than 20 caverns. There are tours of Cas-cade Cave, X Cave, and Saltpetre Cave. Laurel and Horn Hollow caves may be explored without a guide, but a permit is required.

A creek still flows through **Cascade Cave**—deafeningly so in the spring—and the cave's main feature is a 30-foot underground waterfall. One section of the cavern presents an unusual combination of sandy beach, partially exposed lake, and craggy rooms. At one time the cave was lit by artificial lighting virtually around the clock, and the walls became encrusted with moss. Now, many of the walls again are bare and show the interplay of white limestone with the grays and browns of clay and sandstone. Eighteen acres of land above Cascade Cave are a state nature preserve protecting two species that generally grow in cooler climates to the north: shrublike mountain maple and the Canadian yew, a shrubby evergreen.

Another major feature and preserve within the park is Bat Cave, once inhabited in winter by 100,000 Indiana myotis (also known as the social myotis), a species on the federal list of endangered species. Now, some 38,000 bats, about 10 percent of the entire known population, hibernate there every year starting in October. During the winter, if they are disturbed enough to become active, they can exhaust their energy reserves and will not survive into the spring. Thus, there are no scheduled tours of Bat Cave during hibernation.

Seven trails lead to bridges and other natural features. Next to the park is **Tygart State Forest❖,** and linking both of them with Jenny Wiley National Recreation Trail is **Simon Kenton Trail❖,** a strenuous nine-mile backpacking trail named for a scout who is credited with saving Daniel Boone's life.

DANIEL BOONE NATIONAL FOREST: GORGING ON BOONE'S ROCKS AND TREES

West of Carter Caves, near Morehead, Interstate 64 crosses the northern neck of **Daniel Boone National Forest❖,** which includes most of the remaining sites in this chapter. Running northeast to southwest, the national forest spans 140 miles on the western edge, or Pottsville Escarpment, of the Cumberland Plateau, and encompasses 682,000 acres of rolling hills and sandstone bluffs, as well as towns, state parks, pre-

OVERLEAF: *In Daniel Boone National Forest, hikers discover unexpectedly delightful spots; at Dog Slaughter Falls on Dog Slaughter Creek, one can cool off, rest the weary feet, and ponder the origins of place names.*

ABOVE: *Signaling spring in Boone's woodlands and swamps are the pink-splattered painted trillium (left) and the jack-in-the-pulpit (right).* RIGHT: *A waterfall created Rock Bridge in Red River Gorge by eroding the underlying rock and leaving harder upper layers to span the creek.*

serves, and other enclaves within its 21 counties. A separate section, known as the Redbird Purchase Unit for the river that flows through its middle, is east of the main forest and north of Pine Mountain.

Daniel Boone explored this territory, but it is doubtful that even he knew the extent of its riches: within its far-flung boundaries are rushing streams and rivers, numerous plant and animal species, as well as canyons, ancient arches, and natural bridges. Travel by foot and by car is circuitous to say the least. Information and assistance can be obtained ahead of time at the U.S. Forest Service headquarters in Winchester, on Route 89 southeast of Lexington, and within the forest at several district offices. Ask directions elsewhere, too, for it is easy to get sidetracked.

More adventuresome hikers will relish an excursion along the 261-mile **Sheltowee Trace National Recreation Trail❖,** which runs through steep canyons and along rocky ridgetops the length of the national forest, from Route 377 north of Morehead to Tennessee's Pickett State Park. Along the way it connects with 235 miles of trails within the

forest and with other major trail systems, such as the Jenny Wiley to the east and those in the Big South Fork area in Tennessee. At first the trace seems to have escaped that Kentuckian urge to incorporate Boone's name into practically everything, but in fact it too is named for the intrepid—and seemingly ubiquitous—pioneer. Captured by the Shawnee near Blue Licks in 1778 and held for four months, Boone received the nickname Sheltowee, or Big Turtle, from Chief Black Fish.

South of Morehead is **Cave Run Lake,** created by the U.S. Army Corps of Engineers to help control the water quality of the Licking River. **Zilpo Road National Scenic Byway** winds for more than nine miles along ridges in the picturesque countryside surrounding this 8,000-acre recreational lake. The byway (Forest Road 918) can be entered at Zilpo Recreation Area off Forest Service Road 129 about four miles south of Salt Lick. Signs along the road interpret modern forest management methods, Native American life, the pioneer experience, and the once-flourishing iron industry, which at one time gobbled up three acres of

109

ABOVE: *The rising sun paints the top of Natural Bridge a bright gold. This sandstone arch, one of the largest on the Cumberland Plateau,*

forest a day to create charcoal to heat its furnaces.

Among the most striking and well-known sections of the Daniel Boone National Forest is **Red River Gorge Geological Area✣**, 26,000 acres of spectacular erosion, where softer rock has worn away and left a resistant sandstone capstone known as Rockcastle conglomerate. Luckily the gorge, which is about 25 miles long, was spared from a U.S. Army Corps of Engineers dam in the 1960s and 1970s. Today 36 miles of trails traverse this rugged land that contains, according to various sources, more than 80 natural bridges, arches, and tunnels, a plentitude rivaled only by Tennessee's Big South Fork and Utah's Arches National Park. The gorge is also home to innumerable rock houses and lighthouses that, through water and wind erosion, will probably become natural bridges as well.

Among the many dazzling geological phenomena here are Sky Bridge, a completed arch, and Chimney Top, nature's rendition of a theater-in-the-round, providing striking views on three sides—of Courthouse Rock, Raven Rock, and Half Moon Rock—as the Red River, a National Wild and Scenic River, rushes by some 500 feet below. The drive to the trail to Chimney Top is typical of the winding routes in the area: south of Slade, leave the Mountain Parkway and

110

may be a million years old. Up close (above at right) its sculpted and pocked base invites geological inquiries and artistic appreciation.

go to Route 11; almost immediately turn east onto Route 15, proceed seven miles, then turn left or north on Route 715, which leads to Chimney Top Road. Despite all the bare rock, trails through the gorge generally run through heavily wooded areas of hardwoods or pines interspersed with hemlock coves and bigleaf magnolias. More than 500 species of flora include Cranefly orchid, trillium, dogwood, mistflower, cinnamon fern, mayapple, New York fern, prickly holly, smilax, blueberry, striped wintergreen, bloodroot, mountain laurel, fire pink, yellow star grass, rhododendron, and partridgeberry.

Abutting and enhancing the seemingly endless Red River Gorge is the neighboring and even more remote 13,300-acre **Clifty Wilderness**❖ on the east. Added to the National Wilderness Preservation System in 1985, the wilderness now protects more than 750 different flowering plants and 170 species of moss. Although some of the gorge's ridgetop trails may seem relatively easy, the U.S. Forest Service warns that in Clifty Wilderness "significant woods skills are needed to access and use this…rugged

---

OVERLEAF: *In late fall, with most hardwood trees bereft of their foliage, the awesome immensity of the Red River Gorge reverberates with Wendell Berry's words of "haunted places" and "ancient tribesmen."*

ABOVE: *Ever alert, a doe and her two fawns browse on meadow vegetation. Deer give birth in spring, often to twins; if danger arises, the fawns follow their mother's uplifted white tail to safety.*

RIGHT: *A flowering dogwood, its white petal-like bracts underscoring the tree's nearly horizontal branches, adorns the green understory of a hardwood forest in Daniel Boone National Forest.*

pocket of cliffs, bluffs, steep canyons, rocky creeks...."

After driving, climbing, and ambling around the craggy Red River Gorge, any place carrying the label State Resort Park might sound tame. Nevertheless, **Natural Bridge State Resort Park❖,** immediately to the south of Slade on Route 11 off the Mountain Parkway, offers one of the most renowned natural arches in the area. A sandstone arch 65 feet high and 78 feet long, Natural Bridge is one of the largest on the Cumberland Plateau and has been a tourist attraction since the Kentucky Union Railway ran a spur line here for timber speculation more than a century ago. (The railroad donated the lands to the state in 1926.) The 2,000-acre park has nine nature trails up to eight miles long that wander among its unusual natural features. Like a giant sculpture teetering on a dwarfed plinth, Balanced Rock, for instance, is a massive block of sandstone whose base has eroded to barely a quarter the diameter of its flat top.

The park's namesake structure, which may be as much as a million years old, and nearly 1,000 surrounding acres have been dedicated as a state nature preserve, allowing the terrain to remain virtually untouched as an example of the cliff section of the Cumberland Plateau. The area also provides a protected habitat for the federally endangered Virginia big-eared bat, Rafinesque's big-eared bat, and several plant species threatened in the state: sweet pinesap, grass pink (an orchid), and small yellow lady's slipper.

This is a good point to detour out of the national forest to commune with the spirit of Daniel Boone. Head to **Pilot Knob State Nature Preserve❖** almost three miles north of the Mountain Parkway on Brush Creek Road near Clay City. An arduous mile-and-a-half trek takes the hiker to the summit of Pilot Knob. It was from here that the intrepid explorer first gazed over miles and as he later noted "saw with pleasure the beautiful level of Kentucke." Even with an elevation of only 730 feet, Pilot Knob provides a panorama that encompasses the Bluegrass to the west, the Cumberland Plateau to the east, and the surrounding Knobs region. The rock here is so hard that pioneers split and shaped millstones from boulders that tumbled off the top.

Back in Daniel Boone National Forest the treasures continue in the steep, rugged, and remote **Mill Creek❖, Cane Creek❖,** and **Beaver Creek❖** wildlife management areas, which have no developed facilities. Mill Creek covers more than 13,000 acres and is 2 miles south of McKee along the Rockcastle River; Cane Creek covers more than 6,500 acres and is 15 miles west of London along Wood Creek Lake; and Beaver Creek has more than 17,000 acres and can be accessed a mile north of Greenwood on Bauer A Road off Route 27.

East of London, the **Redbird Crest Trail❖** runs for 66 miles

115

through parts of the national forest's separate Redbird Purchase Unit. The Red Bird River courses through the center of these lands, as do the Middle Fork and South Fork of the Kentucky River.

Those with an interest in history may want to retrace pioneer steps at **Levi Jackson State Park❖** on Route 25 southeast of London, midway between the two sections of the national forest. Eight miles of trails encompass portions of Boone's Trace and its successor, the Wilderness Road, trod by more than 200,000 settlers heading west. McHargue's Mill displays a large collection of millstones, and the Mountain Life Museum exhibits old log houses, agricultural tools, and household implements. Levi Jackson was the first judge in Laurel County.

CUMBERLAND FALLS: MOONBOW

Fittingly, this circuit of the Cumberland Plateau returns to Daniel Boone National Forest and a visit to **Cumberland Falls State Resort Park❖,** 20 miles southwest of Corbin on Route 90. Here the 125-foot-wide waterfall, which plunges a spectacular 68 feet, creates a nighttime rendition of a rainbow when the light of a full moon mingles with mist rising from the base of the falls. This moonbow, as it is known, is not as bright as a full daytime rainbow, but its white downstream arch is indeed luminous. The night must be clear and the wind just right, so every visitor does not see a moonbow. But it is worth waiting for, because the only other known example occurs at Victoria Falls in Zimbabwe.

Cumberland Falls itself has inched 45 miles upstream in the millions of years that the rushing Cumberland River has been wearing away its cliff. Water erodes the softer rocks under the capstone, which left unsupported eventually breaks off and plunges into the river below. In 1930, the T. Coleman Dupont family purchased the falls and about 540 acres for the state, ending a six-year dispute over a proposed dam that would have affected one of Kentucky's major natural attractions.

The signature falls and 1,294 of the park's 1,650 acres are now a state nature preserve, which has curtailed the development of more lodging facilities. This designation also protects several species of rare

---

LEFT: *Located in a state park in southeastern Kentucky, Cumberland Falls is the best-known waterfall in the state, casting a spell of wonderment even without the nocturnal appearance of its famed moonbow.*

ABOVE: *The endangered green salamander, which climbs about steep cliffs at night, is one of many rare species at Cumberland Falls.*
RIGHT: *In autumn, a colorful field of sumac turns scarlet in the Bear Creek area of the Big South Fork National River and Recreation Area.*

plants and animals, including the Cumberland bean pearly mussel, which is on the federal endangered-species list; elktoe and fluted kid-neyshell mussels; eastern woodrat and green salamander; and box huckleberry, brook saxifrage, riverweed, and goat's rue. Seventeen miles of trails wind through the woods, gorges, and sandstone cliffs to Cumberland Falls, Eagle Falls, and other sites. A delightful nature trail was built by the Civilian Conservation Corps in 1933. Several other trails connect the park with the 251-mile Sheltowee Trace, which even-tually enters the **Big South Fork National River and Recreation Area** to the southwest. Most of the Big South Fork lands lie across the border in Tennessee, but a very interesting deep gorge and old mining community can be visited on the Kentucky side (see Chapter Six).

From Cumberland Gap to Cumberland Falls, the circuit of Ken-tucky's Cumberland Plateau is complete.

OVERLEAF: *Dense green forests border the Big South Fork of the Cum-berland River as it winds through southeastern Kentucky to Tennessee. The Cumberland then returns to Kentucky, emptying into the Ohio.*

CENTRAL AND WESTERN KENTUCKY:
ZIGZAGGING WESTWARD

W hereas eastern Kentucky is homogeneously mountainous and Appalachian to its craggy core, central and western Kentucky are delightfully diverse, with terrain that ranges from rolling hills to coastal plains, and wildlife that extends from bison to catfish.

Determining whether a site is natural enough to earn a place on this itinerary is especially difficult here. Not included are numerous artificial lakes and state parks that cater nearly exclusively to recreational activities, as well as several wildlife management areas that are focused almost solely around hunting. Sites that are unfettered enough to provide hiking opportunities through interesting forests, gorges, or river bottomlands are included, as are places that have an unusual natural feature, such as a waterfall. Also mentioned are artificial lakes noted for attracting a variety of birds and other wildlife.

This tour begins at Dale Hollow Lake along the state's southern border southeast of Glasgow in Kentucky's Pennyrile, a fairly flat area enlivened with occasional hills and outcroppings that occupies about one third of the state. (The region's name comes from a pioneer pronunciation for the pennyroyal, an abundant, blue-flowered herb that was used for seasonings and medicinal purposes.) Heading northeast,

LEFT: *In the stillness of early morning, a southern red oak on the shore of Lake Barkley catches the first rays of the sun in Land Between the Lakes, a scenic peninsula that straddles Kentucky and Tennessee.*

the next stop is the far-flung Lake Cumberland, the shores of which support a park and a wildlife management area.

Still in the limestone Pennyrile area, the tour moves westward to the state's center and Mammoth Cave, the longest cave in the world and now the centerpiece of a national park. Mammoth Cave has been a tourist attraction since 1815, when slaves served as tour guides in the then privately owned caverns. Even those who are not interested in exploring the cave's underground network of huge rooms and narrow passages will enjoy the numerous woodland trails that meander through the meadows and hardwood forests above ground.

Next the route heads east into the Bluegrass area around Lexington, which takes its nickname from the turf that clothes the hilly pastures of the many Thoroughbred horse farms in the state's heartland. Although not actually blue, the grass has a small flower that imparts a bluish hue in the spring.

The tour proceeds north to a couple of sites with mastodon fossils, a zigzag westward to stops along the Ohio River, and visits to The Knobs, with its rocky castlelike features, and John James Audubon's old stomping grounds. The itinerary then jogs south to the Land Between the Lakes west of Hopkinsville. This peninsula between two lakes created by the dammed Cumberland and Tennessee rivers is host to an astonishing wealth and diversity of plants, trees, birds, and other wildlife, including a herd of bison. Both Mammoth Cave and Land Between the Lakes have been designated as international biosphere reserves.

The tour closes with a swing through several wildlife refuges along the Ohio and Mississippi Flyway near the Tennessee border, where rich bottomlands and swamps harbor graceful herons, mysterious bald cypresses, glorious lotus blossoms, majestic bald eagles, and more.

SOUTH-CENTRAL KENTUCKY: DALE HOLLOW TO GREEN RIVER

Reaching the Kentucky-Tennessee border, **Dale Hollow Lake State Park❖** is one of the beautiful multipurpose parks that dot the

---

OVERLEAF: *Eagles Point affords panoramic vistas of the forested islands and peninsulas at Dale Hollow Lake State Park in the Cumberland foothills. The lake was formed by a dam on Tennessee's Obey River.*

RIGHT: *A new blanket of snow, one of the delightful rewards of visiting Kentucky in the off-season, cloaks trees and shrubs bordering Lake Cumberland.*

foothills of the Cumberland Mountains. Its Kentucky entrance is off Route 449 about 12 miles south of Burkesville. The park occupies a large peninsula that juts into the 28,000-acre lake, which was created when the U.S. Army of Corps of Engineers dammed Tennessee's Obey River. Although its administrators boast that a world-record smallmouth bass—weighing 11 pounds, 15 ounces—was caught here, the park offers 14 miles of trails through 3,000 acres of densely wooded valleys, ridges, and meadows in addition to fishing. Wild turkey, grouse, quail, and one of the largest populations of white-tailed deer in Kentucky roam the park and the corps's adjoining **Dale Hollow Wildlife Management Area❖.**

Travelers will find a similar facility 20 miles to the northeast at **Lake Cumberland State Resort Park❖.** The lake was created when Wolf Creek on the meandering Cumberland River was dammed in 1951, about 200 years after Thomas Walker named the river. Cliffs and caves line the 100-mile-long shoreline, some of which is privately owned. Perched on a narrow, 2,791-acre strip on the lake's north side, the park is marked by steep shady ravines and has a four-mile trail through beech, oak, and hickory forests. The U.S. Army Corps of Engineers manages the 35,000-acre **Lake Cumberland Wildlife Management Area❖,** which ranges from sloping creek bottoms to steep ridges in

hardwood forests, and offers hiking and horseback riding trails.

To the northwest, on Route 55 about 15 miles north of Columbia and the Cumberland Parkway, **Green River Lake State Park❖** adjoins the corps's **Green River Wildlife Management Area❖.** A remote and unimproved trail runs from Pikes Ridge through dense hardwood forests. The terrain is generally rolling, with elevations ranging from 600 to 800 feet in the lake area to nearly 1,000 feet along ridges.

MAMMOTH IN MANY WAYS
Most of Kentucky's 4,000 caves lie in the central-western part of the state in what geologists call the Mississippian Plateau, a region of karst

ABOVE: *The aboveground features of Mammoth Cave National Park rival its subterranean attractions. Among the birds inhabiting its woodlands is the barred owl, which preys on frogs, crayfish, and small mammals.*

topography characterized by sinkholes, underground streams and rivers, and caves. The most famous are the caverns at **Mammoth Cave National Park**❖ northeast of Bowling Green. With a labyrinth of known underground passageways approaching 400 miles in length, the cave is by far the longest in the world, and geologists estimate another 200 miles of passageways are still undiscovered.

Mammoth Cave, however, was not named for its length but for the vast size of some of its chambers—the Rotunda, Snowball Room, and Grand Central Station—which are very impressive to first-time visitors. It is the interplay between large rooms and narrow, tight passageways such as Fat Man's Misery, however, that epitomizes the "what's around the corner" allure that energizes cave explorers.

Although Mammoth Cave does have some decorative stalactites, stalagmites, and drapery formations created by droplets of water falling vertically, it consists mostly of open passageways created as streams and rivers run horizontally in limestone layers below the harder, more resistant sandstone layer. As rainwater seeps into the soil and down sinkholes into the limestone, it becomes mildly acidic and slowly dis-

ABOVE: *In the national park, the green-backed heron (left) patrols the fertile Green River wetlands, while the pileated woodpecker (right), with its distinctive scarlet crest, sticks to the forest and its edges.*

solves channels in the limestone. Constantly seeking lower levels, gradually the water vacates passageways, or caves. Here at Mammoth, below the cave tour routes, the water continues to sculpt new passageways 360 feet underground as it runs off into the Green River.

Mammoth's attributes are indeed mammoth. About 130 forms of life coexist within the cave, making it the most diverse cave ecosystem in the world. A rich variety of animals and approximately 900 flowering plant species populate the meadows and hardwood forests on the surface. And the Green River, into which all the water flows, is one of the most biologically diverse rivers in North America, with 82 fish species and more than 50 species of freshwater mussels, 7 of which are endangered.

Because the cave extends beyond the boundary of the 53,000-acre park and because water affects wildlife habitats on the surface and

OVERLEAF: *Visitors are dwarfed by one of Mammoth Cave's prime features, the Frozen Niagara, a 75-foot-high wall of resplendent flowstone. The full extent of the cave, the longest in the world, is still unknown.*

within the cave and river, the National Park Service is greatly concerned about protecting this world heritage site and international biosphere reserve against pollution. Here children and adults can see and learn firsthand about interrelationships between life above and below ground, from wild turkeys and wood ducks to eyeless cave shrimp and fish no bigger than a finger.

More than ten cave tours are offered seasonally, ranging from a 30-minute introduction to 6.5 hours of crawling, climbing, and squeezing. The two-hour Historic Tour covers two miles of passages explored by Native Americans, an area mined for saltpeter in the early 1800s, large halls, and tight passages. Another two-hour tour takes in pits, domes, decorative stalactites and stalagmites, and the Frozen Niagara, a 50-foot-wide by 75-foot-high wall of lustrous flowstone, one of the cave's outstanding features. Reservations are recommended in the summer and on weekends and holidays, and bring a coat or sweater, for the temperature in the cave hovers around 54 degrees Fahrenheit.

Less visited but certainly as appealing are the park's more than ten miles of trails that wind through magnificent woodlands near the visitor center down to springs flowing from the cave into the Green River. On the north side of the river, 60 miles of trails wander through sandstone gorges thick with hemlock, yellow birch, umbrella magnolia, and holly, as well as a 300-acre remnant of an old-growth forest of yellow poplar, sugar maple, and American beech.

The national park is a wonderful place for bird-watching. Among the more than 200 species sighted are the pileated woodpecker, scarlet tanager, blue heron, barred owl, great horned owl, and 37 kinds of warblers. Mammals most commonly seen are deer, chipmunks, raccoon, and squirrels, but look for coyotes, muskrats, opossums, beavers, and red foxes. Mammoth Cave is accessible from Interstate 65; exit at Park City for the southern entrance, or at Cave City for the northern entrance.

Immediately north of the park on Route 259 is **Nolin Lake Public Wildlife Area❖,** a U.S. Army Corps of Engineers 7,600-acre tract that provides additional hiking opportunities through rugged woodlands.

RIGHT: *With acorns puffing out its cheeks, an eastern chipmunk perches on a log set in a clump of lavender asters. Primarily a ground dweller, the chipmunk usually makes its home in an underground burrow.*

The area around Lexington is known as the Heart of the Bluegrass primarily because of its concentration of Thoroughbred horse farms, with their gently rolling pasturelands and stone fences. The healthy, rich soils of central Kentucky are attributed to the underlying limestone, which erodes quickly and acts as a fertilizer.

About 12 miles southeast of Lexington off Route 421, **Raven Run Nature Sanctuary**❖ provides a municipally supported 376-acre retreat from the urban scene amidst palisades of rock 430 million years old. Here Raven Run and Chandler Creek spill down to the majestic Kentucky River in one of three undeveloped limestone gorges in the Bluegrass area. Seven miles of trails wind through woodlands to streams and meadows and a cascading waterfall. More than 300 wildflower species and 200 bird species have been recorded at Raven Run, which is managed by the Lexington-Fayette Urban County Division of Parks and Recreation.

About 30 miles northeast of Lexington, the **Clay Wildlife Management Area**❖ ranges over 4,800 heavily wooded acres that border the Licking River. This steep to rolling site is maintained by the Kentucky Department of Fish and Wildlife Resources for hikers and students as well as hunters and anglers. A small lake nestles in a shallow valley two and a half miles from the entrance, and a gravel road runs deep into the wilderness. Access is eight miles northeast of Carlisle off Route 32.

BLUE LICKS TO LOUISVILLE: SALT LICKS AND MASTODONS

Nearby, on Route 68 between the village of Blue Lick Springs and Piqua, is a site that touches America's history as a nation as well as its ancient natural environment. **Blue Licks Battlefield State Park**❖ commemorates a Revolutionary War battle fought August 19, 1782, almost a year after Yorktown, in which Canadian and Native American troops ambushed Kentucky militiamen and killed about 70 of them. Daniel Boone escaped, but one of his sons was killed and another wounded.

LEFT: *In the early spring, blue-eyed Mary and wild blue phlox carpet open woodlands in Raven Run Nature Sanctuary near Lexington.*
OVERLEAF: *Fossils of extinct mastodons are evidence that Blue Licks was a salt lick and animal gathering place for thousands of years.*

ABOVE: *The shooting star (left), with its backward petals in full display, prefers open forests and meadows. Introduced from China, the black-berry lily (right) has naturalized on roadsides and in woodlands.*

A century later, Blue Licks became a popular resort as visitors arrived to take the waters at its salt springs. Its bottled water was widely sold until 1896 when the lower spring went dry. When a commercial expedition went to find its source, it netted instead a dramatic scientific discovery: The salt lick had once been a gathering point for mastodons and other extinct species that had become mired in the swampland. Excavations have since turned up fossils of a mastodon tusk three feet long and weighing more than a hundred pounds, brachiopods (marine invertebrates with bivalve shells), calcareous worm tubes (ancient worm burrows preserved in calcium carbonate), and trilobites (segmented marine creatures of the Paleozoic era). Between the time of the mastodons and that of the water-sipping people, the salt lick also attracted buffalo, and today the park includes a section of an old buffalo trace that Route 68 follows from north to south across Kentucky.

Blue Licks is part of a 15-acre state nature preserve where Short's goldenrod grows. Similar to other goldenrod, this September-blooming plant, found only here and on some nearby property, was named for Dr. Charles W. Short, a physician and student of botany in the last century. Botanists believe buffalo helped establish the wildflower here by creating sunlit clearings with their trampling and by transporting seeds in their

ABOVE: *The butter-and-eggs plant (left) is a European native that has made itself at home in dry fields and along roads; the grass pink (right), a mauve orchid, often grows in sphagnum moss in bogs.*

heavy coats. Another rare species found along the trace is Great Plains ladies' tresses orchid. A one-mile trail loops down to the Licking River.

Because of their delicate ecology, many Kentucky State Nature Preserves Commission properties require written permission to visit. One that is freely accessible is **Quiet Trails State Nature Preserve❖,** a little jewel of a forest enclave west of Blue Licks that curls down to the Licking River. A bit off the beaten path, the tranquil preserve is on Pugh's Ferry Road about two miles from where Route 1284 passes through Sunrise, which is off Route 27 about ten miles north of Cynthiana. From the start the four-car parking lot and understated entrance sign suggest privacy and contemplation. A network of mowed trails, some lying along heavily wooded ridges and ravines and others leading into clearings, meander through the 110-acre property as it slopes down to the river. Trail names are simple and direct: Cedar, Sassafras, White Tail Rest, and Deep Hollow. The wide diversity of wildflowers, trees, and birds makes Quiet Trails an excellent educational outing, but on a warm July morning it can also be a particularly secluded retreat, shared only by frogs skittering into tiny ponds, butterflies diving and soaring, and birds conversing cautiously.

As the Ohio River arches northward and around Cincinnati, it

141

traces the boundaries of the glaciers' farthest southern advance, and therein presents explanations for several nearby features. The present Ohio, according to the information on a park plaque, "is but a stunted descendant of the mightier Teays River that once dominated the Midwest from its source in the ancient Appalachian hills to its mouth at the Gulf of Mexico, which then extended close to present St. Louis." Ice Age glaciers formed dams that blocked the Teays and created the Ohio when the ice melted and "great volumes of water were forced to find new paths to the sea."

Glaciers also helped to produce the 20- to 40-foot conglomerate cliffs that are the centerpiece of the **Boone County Cliffs State Nature Preserve❖,** located on a tributary of Middle Creek west of Covington near the northern tip of the state. The conglomerate is composed of gravels—some from as far away as northern Canada—deposited as glacial outwash about 700,000 years ago. Well-maintained foot trails wander through a forest of sugar maple, chinquapin oak, red oak, slippery elm, beech, and black locust. Many wildflowers—poppies, wild ginger, corydalis, and blue phlox—flourish in this secluded, 75-acre, hilly preserve. Enter the preserve on Middle Creek Road, west of Interstate 75 and southwest of Burlington, one and a half miles south of Route 18.

As the glaciers moved as far south as the Cincinnati area, mastodons and other animals were forced south, too, and sometimes became mired in oozy bogs near salt licks. **Big Bone Lick State Park❖,** south of Rabbit Hash on Route 338 and about eight miles west of Walton, is just such a place. An indoor museum and a paved, self-guided trail relate the sorry end of mastodons, mammoths, ground sloths, stag moose, and an extinct ancestor of the bison. An outdoor trail displays replicas of the animals and leads to a fetid spring typical of those throughout this area. A buffalo herd is maintained on the property. The bones have been picked clean over the years at this site, which geologist Preston McGrain in *The Geologic Story of Kentucky* calls "the first widely known collecting locality for vertebrate fossils in North America." Native Americans came here to hunt for game and to gather salt from the mineral springs. The first known European explorers and collectors were French military men in 1739. The area fascinated Benjamin Franklin, McGrain says, and Thomas Jefferson sent in what may have been the hemisphere's first organized paleontological expedition.

Although the likelihood of additional discoveries of 10,000-pound prehistoric creatures is scant, the place is still compelling.

The Frankfort Chapter of the Audubon Society and the Frankfort Bird Club annually convene for their Christmas bird count at **John A. Kleber Wildlife Management Area❖.** Some Decembers as many as 100 species have been sighted during the annual 24-hour watch in this 2,200-acre state reserve. Besides birding, there are extensive opportunities for hiking and studying the terrain, which ranges from rocky creek bottoms to narrow ridges and steep hills with a combination of forest, brush, and grasses. Kleber is about 15 miles north of Frankfort, the state capital, and is reached via Route 368, between Routes 127 and 227. The site is managed by the Kentucky Department of Fish and Wildlife Resources.

Also near the state capital is one of those small wildlife sanctuaries that provide important educational programs for school groups and pleasant outings for adults. The **Clyde E. Buckley Wildlife Sanctuary❖,** which covers 275 acres near the Kentucky River, was the National Audubon Society's first sanctuary in the central United States. It is located on Germany Road in Millville about six miles west of Route 60. Well-marked paths wind through a transition forest, which is home to plants and animals that generally live both farther north and farther south. Buckley shelters some 100 bird species and a larger number of wildflowers, including yellow corydalis, white trout lily, bloodroot, wild ginger, and dwarf larkspur. Among its tree species are Ohio buckeye, honey locust, sugar maple, black walnut, slippery elm, wild black cherry, shagbark hickory, and the tulip poplar. It also boasts a chinquapin oak more than a century old.

Those tracking Kentucky's courageous frontiersman may wish to visit the graves of Daniel and Rebecca Boone in the Frankfort Cemetery overlooking the city and the Kentucky River.

To the west and south, between Frankfort and Louisville, **Taylorsville Lake Wildlife Management Area❖** adjoins **Taylorsville Lake State Park❖** along Routes 55 and 44 about ten miles north of the Blue-

---

OVERLEAF: *The setting sun casts a golden sheen over the still waters of Taylorsville Lake. The surrounding park and wildlife area provide a woodland home to a wide variety of birds and small mammals.*

grass Parkway. The lake and more than 11,000 acres of wooded hillsides ranging from gently sloping to steep are home to otters, deer, and wild turkeys and also serve as a waterfowl refuge during the winter.

Near Louisville is **Six Mile Island State Nature Preserve❖,** a cigar-shaped island in the Ohio River that has become a haven for various waterfowl displaced by urban growth. Once used as farmland, the preserve is being allowed to revert to its wild state as a riverine island ecosystem. Silver maples, cottonwoods, sycamores, and other trees have reestablished themselves. Accessible by boat, Six Mile Island is one and a half miles upstream from the Cox Park boat ramp along River Road on the Louisville side of the river.

THE KNOBS AND PENNYRILE

The 14,000 acres of the **Bernheim Arboretum and Research Forest❖,** in The Knobs belt around the Bluegrass, constitute a superb combination of museum and natural habitat. About 25 miles south of Louisville and 15 miles west of historic Bardstown on Route 245, the forest is owned by the Isaac W. Bernheim Foundation (named for the man who purchased the original tract in 1929), which over the years has restored overharvested woodlands to nearly natural states. Tower Hill Road and Paul's Point Loop lead visitors to the trailheads of 14 hiking trails. The roadsides are well-mowed and the trailheads clearly visible, but once on the trails, the impression of manicured parkland is left behind. On a summer day a red-tailed hawk may circle overhead, seemingly tracking a hiker through the lush woods that harbor Virginia pine, yellow poplar, sawtooth oak, American beech, sugar maple, American elm, and white ash. Near the entrance an arboretum covers 250 acres of wide meadows with concentrations of planted and labeled trees and shrubs. In gardens near Lake Nevin grow Clavey's dwarf honeysuckle, Russian cypress ground cover, Mongolian linden, rose campion, yellow patrina, moonbeam threadleaf coreopsis, Japanese maple and larch, and the puffy smoketree.

Tracking back northwest to the Ohio River, we come to **Yellow-**

RIGHT: *Spring busts out at Bernheim Forest, which includes 10,000 acres of restored woodlands. Among the trees, the purplish-pink petals of eastern redbuds contrast with the emerging leaves of a yellow poplar.*

bank Wildlife Management Area❖ on the edge of a region that extends from south-central Kentucky. Known as the Pennyrile, its name is a pioneer corruption of pennyroyal, the abundant herb that is fairly common in the state. (Early settlers used the mint as a seasoning and for medicinal purposes, and it remains a home remedy today.) Yellowbank WMA, which occupies 6,000 acres along Route 259 about 20 miles north of Hardinsburg and 20 miles west of Brandenburg, has miles of old roads suitable for hiking; the terrain ranges from steep and moderate slopes of hardwoods to river-bottom farmlands. While Yellowbank is mostly wild, part of one tract is a self-guided habitat restora-

ABOVE: *American artist and ornithologist John James Audubon (1785–1851) lived in Henderson, Kentucky, for 9 years and spent more than 30 years observing wildlife. Among his bird and mammal portraits is this watercolor of a pair of buffleheads, the smallest of all North American ducks, which still migrate through the area.*

LEFT: *An oak spreads its mighty arms beside Scenic Lake in the John James Audubon State Park in Henderson.*

tion demonstration area including prairie grasses and wetlands. Yellowbank Creek provides access to the Ohio River.

HENDERSON: WHERE AUDUBON ROAMED

The mere mention of Audubon seems to conjure up images of restful forests trilling with the sounds of birds. **John James Audubon State Park❖** and the adjoining state nature preserve fulfill the promise inherent in the name of the artist and ornithologist, who was captivated by the avian species prevalent in this section of the Mississippi Flyway. Audubon lived in Henderson on the Kentucky-Indiana border from 1810 to 1819, and some of the lands where he roamed and sketched are protected along Route 41 on Henderson's north side.

Heavy use necessitated that about half of the park's 700 acres be

149

dedicated as a state nature preserve in 1979 in an attempt to leave these forests on rich loess hills near the Ohio River in as nearly a natural state as possible. The preserve's primary purpose is to protect the area and educate visitors. Those who stroll the Wilderness Lake, Back-country, and Lake Overlooks trails have many opportunities to observe a variety of plants and animals.

Near the park entrance a museum displays Audubon watercolors, engravings, and memorabilia. Here, too, is the trailhead for a short loop where signs interpret such treasures as a pin oak with a 40-inch diameter that was a mere sapling when young Audubon was enchanted by these woods.

Throughout the Wolf Hills area, which includes the park, two forest communities prevail: beech and sugar basswood in the moist, rich northern portion, and oak, sugar maple, and tulip tree in the drier southern section. More than 60 tree species are found in this climax forest, and nearly 300 wildflower species decorate the woods, where fallen trees are left to decay and nourish countless plant communities. In some ravines, they stack up like old split-rail fences.

A visit to the woods in mid July finds the morning light slanting down on banks of periwinkle, creating a deceptive sheen as if the plants had magically sprouted white summer buds to replace their faded purplish blossoms. Around a turn and down a bank, the little lake spreads its carpet of green ooze. Boots on

ABOVE: *A nimble masked bandit, the raccoon spends nights on the prowl, wading in streams for turtles, crayfish, and frogs, or combing the woods for nuts, berries, and small mammals.*
RIGHT: *A picturesque waterfall spills over a moss-covered ledge into a small pool in Pennyrile State Forest, a quiet retreat northwest of Hopkinsville, Kentucky.*
OVERLEAF: *Bright orange in dawn's early light, feathery wetland grasses brighten autumnal Long Creek Wildlife Refuge, home to more than 25 species of waterfowl at Land Between the Lakes.*

Left: *A female river otter and two youngsters strike a seemingly choreographed pose on a wetland log. Aquatic acrobats, otters dive, float, play tag, and belly flop down riverbanks.*

Right: *Layers of ancient limestone form the shoreline of Kentucky Lake. Before two dams were built, the rocky peninsula now called Land Between the Lakes was known as the moonshine capital of the world.*

the boardwalk herald an intruder, and birds scatter, leaving only butterflies and dragonflies. Yet the 130 species of birds in the park's registry—among them snow goose, bufflehead, kingfisher, saw-whet owl, and 20 kinds of warblers—should have no complaint about humans, for it was Audubon who helped perpetuate them and perhaps saved some species from the fate of the stuffed passenger pigeon in a glass case back at Bernheim Forest. Picturing Audubon sketching deftly and with passion here as he spotted a bobwhite or a fox sparrow is perhaps more pleasant than recalling the irrefutable evidence that Audubon, the great observer and recorder of avian life, was also an accomplished taxidermist.

Jumping about 40 miles south, beyond the Western Kentucky Parkway and Dawson Springs, **Pennyrile Forest State Resort Park**❖ and the adjacent **Pennyrile State Forest**❖ provide more than 8 miles of marked trails and two lakes within their more than 15,000 acres. The two places are named for the wild pennyroyal mint, which grows there from July to September.

LAND BETWEEN THE LAKES

More than 200 miles of hiking trails and some 400 miles of roads wind through the 170,000 acres of **Land Between the Lakes**❖. The park received its name because it occupies a long, scenic peninsula defined when the Tennessee Valley Authority dammed a section of the Tennessee River in 1945 and then a section of the Cumberland River in 1965, creating Kentucky Lake to the west and Lake Barkley to the east. At 160,000 acres, Kentucky Lake is the largest artificial

lake in the eastern United States; a canal to the north of the park connects the two lakes and rivers. The peninsula itself, once called Land Between the Rivers, is 40 miles long and 6 to 8 miles wide; it has 4 small interior lakes and 300 miles of shoreline. About 60 percent of this land lies in Kentucky, the rest in Tennessee. The TVA's Golden Pond Visitor Center and Planetarium, midway between Hopkinsville and Mayfield, is reached via Routes 68 and 80.

Land Between the Lakes and a surrounding two million acres were designated an international biosphere reserve in 1991 because they epitomized an interior low-plateau biogeographical province with a natural core, a buffer zone, and a transition zone. The reasons for this special recognition quickly become apparent.

Among the 250 species of birds in the area are raptors such as the bald eagle, which has been restored as a year-round nesting species in recent years, and several kinds of hawks and owls. Within the rolling woodlands and the wetlands grow more than 800 floral species and a great variety of trees: red oak, black oak, sugar maple, hickory, basswood, sycamore, ash, elm, river birch, white oak, sweet gum, persimmon, and red mulberry. Each spring the pastel blossoms of dogwood, serviceberry, crab apple, plum, and redbud brighten the woods and delicate spangle grass, drooping sedge, and various ferns and wildflowers carpet the ground.

The largest publicly owned herd of bison east of the Mississippi roams a 200-acre preserve on the peninsula. In addition to large populations of wild turkey and white-tailed deer, which are common throughout Kentucky, Land Between the Lakes has fallow deer, introduced European-Asian natives that range in color from solid white to nearly black.

The 65-mile North-South Trail winds through valleys, along streams and lakeshores, and by historic homesteads on old logging roads and fire roads. (Shelters for backpackers are located every 15 miles.) In addition, a series of loop trails follows General Ulysses S. Grant's 1862 route through rugged hills from Fort Henry on the Tennessee River to Fort Donelson on the Cumberland River. Look for beavers, river otters, and waterfowl from two wildlife observation points on Hematite Lake Trail; endangered red wolves and a number of indigenous birds and mammals are in residence at the Nature Station.

Although there are no commercial facilities on the peninsula, Land Be-

ABOVE: *Perched on a thistle blossom, a viceroy butterfly displays its tawny coloring and white-spotted black borders. Birds avoid the viceroy because it resembles the monarch, which they find distasteful.*

tween the Lakes is surrounded and supported by a network of resorts and marinas and by separate state parks, which also offer hiking opportunities amid the wetlands and along the modest bluffs of the Tennessee and Cumberland rivers. To the east is **Lake Barkley State Resort Park❖** on Routes 68 and 80 west of Cadiz. To the immediate west of the central entrance to Land Between the Lakes, also along Routes 68 and 80, is **Kenlake State Resort Park❖,** and at the northern end of Land Between the Lakes is **Kentucky Dam Village State Resort Park❖** along Routes 62 and 641 south of Gilbertsville. A mile and a half long and more than 200 feet high, the nearby Kentucky Dam is the TVA's largest.

WEST TO THE MISSISSIPPI: REFUGES ALONG THE FLYWAY

Somehow the presence of nearby cornfields does not destroy a sense of remoteness that pervades 2,150-acre **Kaler Bottoms Wildlife Management Area❖,** a Kentucky Department of Fish and Wildlife Resources tract eight miles northeast of Mayfield between Routes 131 and 408 and Tim Owen Road. Often inaccessible during rainy periods, this

157

primitive cypress swamp serves as a rookery for blue herons and home to raccoon, swamp rabbits, and deer. A visit to Kaler Bottoms in mid-August finds the black-and-orange viceroy butterflies so common in Kentucky and the intricate purplish blue passion-flower blossoms in their final phases.

The **Metropolis Lake State Nature Preserve❖**, a 123-acre gem seven miles west of Paducah, encompasses one of the few existing natural lakes in the Ohio River floodplain. Follow Route 60 from where it intersects with Interstate 24 at Paducah, then turn north on Route 996 and go five miles to the unmarked entrance on the right. A path leads close to the 50-acre lake through woodlands flourishing with bald cypress and swamp tupelo and by stands of common papaw, whose pendulous leaves suggest the tropics. The warty hackberry tree and the shagbark hickory are also found here. Beavers and river otters frequent this secluded little enclave, as do white-tailed deer, wild turkeys, and box turtles. Spangle grass, purple rocket, and valerian grace the woodland floor.

Along the top of the lake at the entrance to **Ballard County Wildlife Management Area❖** lies a vast stand of lotuses, their great leaves shaped like old Victrolas, their golden white blossoms luminous against the mossy water. Covering more than 8,000 acres, Ballard is one of several state fish and wildlife resources areas along the

ABOVE: *The American lotus, with its fragrant pale yellow flowers, shrouds quiet pools along the Mississippi River and related waterways. Its spectacular umbrellalike leaves are often two feet wide.*

Ohio River within the Mississippi Flyway. No trails service this vast complex of wetlands and marshes, but hunting roads, forested areas, and 11 lakes are open to the public. Although the marshy bottomlands and lakes lie amid grainfields and campsites, there are plenty of dense forests away from civilization to explore. On a hot August day, vivid cardinal flowers, a spider lily in full bloom, and a plethora of pristine white blossoms of the wild potato vine may be among the many wildflowers spotted. Look here for great blue herons, white-tailed deer, wild turkeys, swamp rabbits, and river otters. Besides wintering bald eagles, other federally threatened or endangered species at Ballard include the interior least tern and orange-footed pimpleback mussel. State threatened and endangered species include the evening bat, hooded merganser, and spotted sunfish. The area, which is closed from October 15 through March 15, can be approached via Route 60 to La Center, then Routes 358, 1105, and 473.

Similar fish and wildlife facilities in the area are **Peal Wildlife Man-**

agement Area❖, a 2,119-acre marshlands and river bottomland tract with entrances west of Barlow on Mounds City Landing Road, and west of Wickliffe on Route 60; **Swan Lake Wildlife Management Area❖,** 2,536 acres six miles northwest of Wickliffe on Route 60; and **Winford Wildlife Management Area❖,** six miles northwest of Bardwell on Route 62. Swan Lake, like Ballard, has 11 lakes; the largest was named by John James Audubon in 1810 after he observed trumpeter swans there. This area is closed from October 15 through March 15 to serve as a winter refuge for migratory birds such as double-crested cormorants, bald eagles, and ring-billed and herring gulls. Of special note at the 237-acre Winford tract is a summer swath of vivid yellow partridge peas that grows between wheel tracks leading to a placid lake. Interspersed among them are tall rose mallow flowers, whose potent nectar draws forth efficient squadrons of hungry bumblebees.

Although closed in places by the devastating floods of 1993, the Great River Road pays homage to the nearby Mississippi River with a variety of views from Canada to the Gulf of Mexico. Along the route south, in the town of Columbus, is **Columbus-Belmont State Park❖,** which commemorates a Civil War action in which the Confederates stretched a huge chain and anchor across the river in an attempt to block Union gunboats. Although the park is devoted largely to the war, its two miles of trails provide impressive vistas of the great river that has figured so prominently in America's natural and human history.

Farther south, along the river in Fulton County, the state reaches its lowest elevation, 257 feet, and even farther south is a small portion of **Reelfoot Lake National Wildlife Refuge❖,** most of which is in Tennessee (see Chapter Five). Also on the border, to the far southwest, is a geographical oddity, a bit of Kentucky that can be reached by motor vehicle only by driving through Tennessee on Route 22. The isthmus at New Madrid was created by a bend in the Mississippi and today is mostly agricultural lands. New Madrid itself is across the river in Missouri.

As for the next chapter and tour, suffice it to say that the story behind New Madrid and Lake Reelfoot is earth-shaking.

OVERLEAF: *A beaver lodge built among bald cypress trees, ghostly reflections in still waters, a hint of emerging vapors: all heighten the inherent mystery of Reelfoot Lake on the Kentucky-Tennessee border.*

TENNESSEE

PART THREE

T E N N E S S E E

If a sixth grader came home from school and told of studying a place that included, from west to east, a coastal plain related to the Atlantic Ocean, a rim around a basin of karst topography, a wide plateau, and major mountains and valleys, parents might assume that the child was learning about part of Europe. Instead, it could be Tennessee.

Shaped like a parallelogram, Tennessee is only about 115 miles from north to south, but it stretches 430 miles from west to east and is characterized by a great topographical and cultural diversity. To most residents, the state is three states in one: West Tennessee, Middle Tennessee, and East Tennessee. And they will argue about where one begins and the other ends until the coffeepot is empty or the iced tea runs out.

Tennessee, however, can be divided and subdivided in all sorts of ways depending on whether a geologist, geographer, tourism official, historian, or average citizen is doing the dividing. Roughly the western third of the state is dominated by the terrain of the coastal plain, a region of alluvial plains and wetlands that stretches west from the Atlantic seaboard generally south of Tennessee and then curves north in a broad band along the Mississippi River as far as the western tip of Kentucky. Tennessee's middle third constitutes the basin of what was once a great inland sea that helped create those plains. The eastern third is dominated by the Cumberland Plateau, the Unakas, and the Great Smoky Mountains, all parts of the Appalachians.

If West Virginia and Kentucky are a mix of the North and South in many ways, Tennessee is more so. Its climate fluctuates between the coolness of the North and the subtropical humidity of the South. Shivering in cold, whipping winds on a great heath bald atop Roan Mountain or 6,200-foot Clingmans Dome seems far removed from enduring a hot summer afternoon swatting gnats along the Chickasaw Bluffs on the Mississippi River. Yet both could occur on a single day in June.

Tennesseans are just as variable and independent as the weather.

PRECEDING PAGES: *At the break of dawn, a clump of trees rises like a phantom ship above the placid waters of Tennessee's Lake Barkley.*

The first European Americans to settle in the area trooped back east over the mountains during the American Revolution to help defeat the British at Kings Mountain in South Carolina. Commemorated today in the Overmountain Victory National Historic Trail, that trek started a tradition that gave Tennessee its nickname, the Volunteer State. Tennesseans volunteered for the War of 1812, fighting victoriously with Andrew Jackson at New Orleans, and they volunteered for the Mexican War in the late 1840s. And when the Civil War erupted, they volunteered on both sides: Tennessee became the last southern state to secede, but thousands of men, especially in East Tennessee, joined the Union cause.

Some residents, however, did not secede voluntarily. The Cherokee, who once claimed a territory that included Kentucky and Tennessee and stretched into West Virginia, Alabama, Georgia, and South Carolina, were driven off their lands and forced to Oklahoma in 1838–39. Although Congressman Davy Crockett opposed this "removal," promoted by then-President Jackson, Crockett was in the minority and could not prevent it. Thousands of members of the Cherokee Nation died on the way west. Today this sad chapter in American history is commemorated in the state's Cherokee National Forest and by the Trail of Tears National Historic Trail, which consists of an 826-mile overland highway route from Chattanooga to Tahlequah, Oklahoma, and a 1,226-mile foot route along major rivers. A small Cherokee reservation adjacent to Great Smoky Mountains National Park is home today to descendants of about 1,000 members of the tribe who hid in the hills.

The national forest and national park are showcases for more than 1,400 plant species that prosper in Tennessee, along with a wide variety of mammals, reptiles, fish, and birds. The forests were so vast that early settlers believed they could be perpetually cut, and the abundance of minerals led to extensive coal mining and some copper mining. With the advent of New Deal conservation programs in the 1930s, much of this ravaging declined. Today the landscape is recovering, and new forests and superb recreational beauty delight the traveler's eye.

For simplicity in touring, this section divides the state into two loops. The first one, Chapter Five, highlights the western and middle parts of Tennessee from the Gulf Coastal Plain to the eastern edge of the Nashville Basin. The second loop in the following chapter covers the Appalachians from the Cumberland Plateau eastward to the North Carolina border.

OVERLEAF: *Alexander Helwig Wyant's romantic but realistic landscape* Tennessee *(1866) is a late Hudson River School tribute to the state.*

WESTERN-MIDDLE TENNESSEE:
GREAT RIVER TO THE BASIN

Tennessee and Kentucky, its neighbor to the north, share not only a common border but also several major rivers. The Cumberland forms in southeastern Kentucky, winds through eastern Tennessee, and returns to Kentucky northwest of Nashville; the Tennessee starts near Knoxville, meanders south into Alabama, and then heads back north across western Tennessee into Kentucky. Both pick up numerous tributaries, are dammed in several places, and empty into the Ohio River, which flows into the Mississippi that snakes south, forming the western border of Kentucky and Tennessee.

To uninitiated travelers, it can be baffling to cross and recross the Tennessee and Cumberland rivers in the course of a single trip. The Mississippi is not as confusing, and it is along this great river—the Big River, the mighty Mississippi—that we begin our trek eastward across Tennessee's coastal plain toward the Highland Rim and the Nashville Basin in the central part of the state. Once the rivers are sorted out, it can also be fun to try defining the dividing line where the bottomland blues of Memphis fades into the country-western tunes of Nashville.

First, a few words about Tennessee's watery heritage. With one exception, all of the state's lakes are artificial, created by dams built

---

LEFT: *Silhouetted against a shimmering green lake, the pink flowers of an eastern redbud herald the arrival of spring in Tennessee. The native redbud thrives in the state's moist valleys and hardwood forests.*

171

by the massively influential Tennessee Valley Authority and Army Corps of Engineers. Established in 1933 under President Franklin D. Roosevelt as a New Deal program, the TVA was formed to curtail the persistent flooding that was destroying communities, to improve river navigation, and to provide hydroelectric power for new industries and to citizens who had never enjoyed its benefits. Extremely productive, the program constructed more than 30 major dams in the Tennessee River watershed, which includes neighboring states.

These itineraries pass many of the TVA dams and their attendant lakes, which have become sanctuaries for wildlife, especially for ducks, geese, and migrating raptors. Some lakes are not covered in this guide because they predominantly emphasize recreation. Many Tennessee wildlife management areas are not included because they are primarily hunting preserves; some appear because they are along the route and have special wildlife viewing possibilities or special conservation programs.

The sites in this Western-Middle Tennessee itinerary are relatively modest in size when compared with the large parks and forests in the eastern part of the state. Although focused around natural history, several of the smaller sites have ties with Native American and pioneer heritage or with the Civil War. Several have bald cypress trees and wildflowers not found or not common in eastern Tennessee. All of them are special.

But what about that one major natural lake? This itinerary will pay it a visit before continuing south along the Mississippi River from Tennessee's northwest corner, then traveling northeast to the state's approximate center around its capital, Nashville.

REELFOOT: A QUAKE, A LAKE

Predating the Tennessee Valley Authority's man-made creations by more than a century, a more potent force, the New Madrid Fault, took a cataclysmic approach to lake construction. In the winter of 1811–12, one of the strongest earthquakes on record sent the countryside along the Mississippi floodplain in northwest Tennessee into a bizarre paroxysm. The ground rolled like ocean waves, leveling vast forests and dropping 8 to 25 feet in some places. The earthquake caused the Mississippi to flow backward for a while, and the river filled the huge void left by the sunken land. The resulting lake submerged parts of the forest, and today dead trees poke above the watery horizon.

172

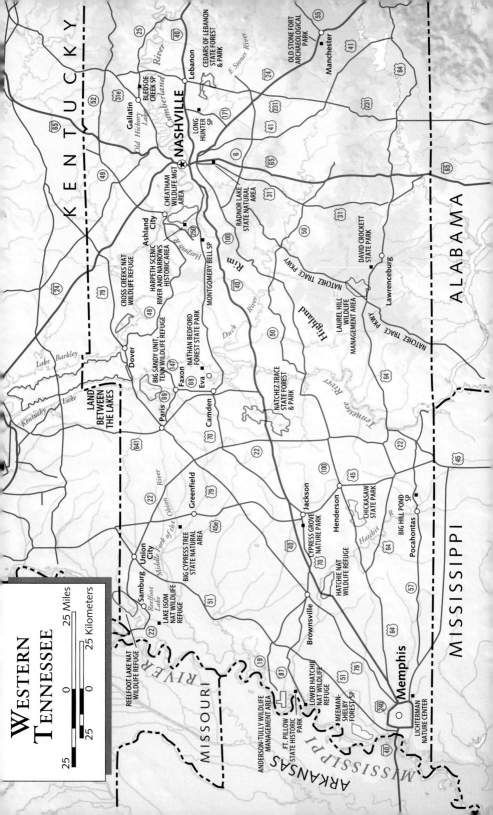

WESTERN TENNESSEE

KENTUCKY

ALABAMA

MISSISSIPPI

ARKANSAS

MISSOURI

NASHVILLE

Memphis

Lebanon

Gallatin

Manchester

Lawrenceburg

Ashland City

Dover

Paris

Camden

Faxon
Eva

Greenfield

Jackson

Henderson

Union City

Samburg

Brownsville

Pocahontas

Cross Creeks Nat Wildlife Refuge

Harpeth Scenic River and Narrows Historic Area

Cheatham Wildlife Mgt Area

Bledsoe Creek SP

Cedars of Lebanon State Forest & Park

Old Stone Fort Archaeological Park

Long Hunter SP

Radnor Lake State Natural Area

Montgomery Bell SP

David Crockett State Park

Natchez Trace State Forest & Park

Nathan Bedford Forest State Park

Big Sandy Unit, Tenn Wildlife Refuge

Laurel Hill Wildlife Management Area

Land Between the Lakes

Lake Barkley

Kentucky Lake

Big Cypress Tree State Natural Area

Cypress Grove Nature Park

Chickasaw State Park

Big Hill Pond SP

Reelfoot Lake Nat Wildlife Refuge

Lake Isom Nat Wildlife Refuge

Hatchie Nat Wildlife Refuge

Anderson-Tully Wildlife Management Area

Ft. Pillow State Historic Park

Lower Hatchie Nat Wildlife Refuge

Meeman-Shelby Forest SP

Lichterman Nature Center

Reelfoot Lake

Old Hickory Lake

Cumberland River

E Stones River

Harpeth River

Duck River

Tennessee River

Obion River

Middle Fork of the Obion River

Hatchie River

Rim

Highland

Natchez Trace Pkwy

25 Miles

25 Kilometers

This new body of water, 5 miles wide and 14 miles long, was named Reelfoot Lake after a legendary Chickasaw with a deformity that caused him to reel as he walked. The gods had consigned him to the bottom of the lake because he had kidnapped the princess of another tribe. Legend or not, the land certainly reeled.

Reelfoot Lake became a flourishing natural fish hatchery, and about 7,000 acres of its wetlands form havens for numerous species. Not surprisingly, the human population disputed over ownership of this sudden landscape feature, and some attempts were even made to drain it. In 1908 matters grew so bad that an attorney for the West Tennessee Land Company, which sought sole possession of the lake, was lynched by vigilantes. The state stepped in, sent the militia, and eventually took possession through public domain.

In the nineteenth century, Jim Bowie and Davy Crockett fished in the lake and hunted in the surrounding woods, and today the place still attracts plenty of anglers and hunters as well as tourists. Fortunately, the **Reelfoot Lake** and **Lake Isom**❖ national wildlife refuges—with headquarters just off Route 22 about 9 miles north of Samburg and 15 miles southwest of Union City—encompass 12,000 acres, ensuring that development is neither rampant nor unplanned.

Located along the Mississippi Flyway, one of four great migration routes between Canada and South America, the refuges attract thousands of migrating and resident birds. In the Grassy Island area, birds whoop and whistle, groves of bald cypress poke their knees above the shallow waters, great blue herons haphazardly wander near the unpaved, russet roadway, and turtles suddenly slide off floating logs as visitors approach.

The Reelfoot-Isom complex is the winter home of 100 to 200 bald eagles, and in the winter, mallards sometimes number as many as 400,000 and Canada geese populations grow to 150,000. Of the 250 bird species sighted, less common ones include osprey, anhinga, screech owl, snowy egret, blue-winged teal, and least bittern. The 53 mammal species include 13 kinds of bats, plus mink, bobcat, and red

---

LEFT: *A trio of bald cypress trees, needle-leaved symbols of western Tennessee's watery domains, thrive at the edge of Reelfoot Lake.*
OVERLEAF: *Among the bald cypress trunks at Reelfoot, a great blue heron stands motionless in the shallows, stalking frogs and fish.*

its second century and the cypr
pierced its aura of permanence.
to the ground, mortally wounde
smoldered for two weeks. The tr
tial attackers for another 16 yea
wind broke off an additional 40 f

Today a sign at the entrance
ply: "The Tree is across the rive
the trail. Tours crossing the r
Though only a ten-foot stump
compasses 330 acres, of which
forest and 30 upland meadowl
the area, frequented by coyote
than a mile twists down to the
east of Reelfoot and 5 miles nor

ON THE MISSISSIPPI

Turning south, the itinerary a
sion of Civil War generals
Chickasaw Bluffs at gunboat

**ABOVE: *Clutching a ba___
displays the white u___
over water, this rapt___***

fox. Amphibians and
graphic ranges of ma___

SOUTH OF REELFO___

Continuing south, t___
July 1976, when the
gratulation over its 2___
ing its ground near
for more than a mi___
State Natural Area___
reached its own p___
Charlemagne's time
William the Conque___
towering—the talle___
tree of any species
measured 13 feet in

In 1,350 years, th___
thunder, and lightni___
30 miles away had
amoral and unsenti___

nize the view today. Since the Civil War, the river's course has migrat-ed westward about a mile through the relatively soft alluvial plain, looping to form an oxbow lake, known as Cold Creek Chute. Without doubt the strategic value of the Chickasaw Bluffs would be much di-minished in battle now. Adding to this gradual erosion was the sud-den slipping of 30 acres into the delta all at once on September 19, 1908. Today the view from Chickasaw Bluff No. 1 finds the mighty Mississippi still dominant but definitely distant.

A section of the Chickasaw Bluffs and a good bit of the old Civil War entrenchments are now part of **Fort Pillow State Historic Park❖** about 50 miles south of the Reelfoot Lake area. Named for General Gideon J Pillow, a hero in the Mexican War, the site is on Route 207 off Route 87, about 17 miles west of Route 51. The 1,650-acre park provides a haven for the red-tailed hawk, wild turkey, bobcat, white-tailed deer, and red fox, and nearly 50 bird species, including the Mississippi kite. Ten miles of trails wind amid woods, Civil War remnants, and along the bluff over-looking the river; a 25-acre man-made lake is surrounded by a wetland marked by beaver dams and a marsh set out with nesting boxes for wood ducks. The park is surrounded by other public facilities with simi-

ABOVE: *A denizen of freshwater swamps and lakes, a long-necked anhinga (left) spreads its wings to dry. Perched on a branch above a wetland, an elegant snowy egret (right) waits for likely prey to appear.*

its second century and the cypress endured in its fourteenth, lightning pierced its aura of permanence. More than 100 feet of the tree careened to the ground, mortally wounded and partially ignited. The fallen giant smoldered for two weeks. The tree's remaining 50 feet mocked its celestial attackers for another 16 years, the blink of an eye, until a violent wind broke off an additional 40 feet. The giant was defeated.

Today a sign at the entrance of Big Cypress Tree SNA explains simply: "The Tree is across the river and has fallen. It cannot be seen from the trail. Tours crossing the river to the tree are by arrangement." Though only a ten-foot stump of its namesake remains, the park encompasses 330 acres, of which about 300 are hardwood bottomland forest and 30 upland meadowland. Some 200 songbird species inhabit the area, frequented by coyote and white-tailed deer. A trail of more than a mile twists down to the river. The park is about 20 miles southeast of Reelfoot and 5 miles northwest of Greenfield off Route 45E.

ON THE MISSISSIPPI

Turning south, the itinerary approaches the Mississippi. The succession of Civil War generals who gazed straight down from the Chickasaw Bluffs at gunboat battles would find it difficult to recog-

nize the view today. Since the Civil War, the river's course has migrat-
ed westward about a mile through the relatively soft alluvial plain,
looping to form an oxbow lake, known as Cold Creek Chute. Without
doubt the strategic value of the Chickasaw Bluffs would be much di-
minished in battle now. Adding to this gradual erosion was the sud-
den slipping of 30 acres into the delta all at once on September 19,
1908. Today the view from Chickasaw Bluff No. 1 finds the mighty
Mississippi still dominant but definitely distant.

A section of the Chickasaw Bluffs and a good bit of the old Civil War
entrenchments are now part of **Fort Pillow State Historic Park❖** about
50 miles south of the Reelfoot Lake area. Named for General Gideon J.
Pillow, a hero in the Mexican War, the site is on Route 207 off Route 87,
about 17 miles west of Route 51. The 1,650-acre park provides a haven
for the red-tailed hawk, wild turkey, bobcat, white-tailed deer, and red
fox, and nearly 50 bird species, including the Mississippi kite. Ten miles
of trails wind amid woods, Civil War remnants, and along the bluff over-
looking the river; a 25-acre man-made lake is surrounded by a wetland
marked by beaver dams and a marsh set out with nesting boxes for
wood ducks. The park is surrounded by other public facilities with simi-

lar Mississippi terrain and wildlife. The **Anderson-Tully Wildlife Management Area❖** lies immediately northeast of Fort Pillow, and **Lower Hatchie National Wildlife Refuge❖** is to the southwest.

So deeply does the Mississippi River course through the sentiment and fact of American history and culture that viewing it can create a sense of anticipation laced with nostalgia. At **Meeman-Shelby Forest State Park❖,** 10 miles north of Memphis, a visitor can approach the great river from up high or down below. Near the river, the flat farmland gives way abruptly to a lush hardwood forest with leafy ravines and beckoning trails, eventually providing glimpses of the river and then open access. Here, no more than a few feet below, the silvery tide glistens along its way to the sights and smells and adventures evoked in composer Ferde Graffe's *Mississippi Suite*. In contrast, from Chickasaw Bluff No. 3 the Mississippi appears as a wide and sweeping panorama. Some 20 miles of hiking and horseback trails offer riverine vistas as well as views of the superb bottomland and upland hardwood forests. More than 60 bird species are listed as passing through or resident at the park.

In Memphis there is a jewel of a park that makes the term urban-natural seem not quite such an oxymoron. **Lichterman Nature Center❖** is closely surrounded by develop-

ABOVE: *At Reelfoot Lake, a swamp rabbit watches for predators. When pursued, this exceptional swimmer can submerge completely, leaving only its nose exposed to breathe.*

LEFT: *A sleek brown mink pauses on a waterside log. These small mammals den along riverbanks and prey on muskrats, turtles, fish, rabbits, and chipmunks.*

ment but remains an enclave of the natural as well as the meticulously planned, managed, and protected. During the early 1940s, the land belonged to Bill Terry, manager of the New York Giants baseball team, and it was sold to the Lichterman and Loewenberg families in 1944. Portions of the land were donated to the city, and in 1983 the center was

181

ABOVE: *Known as a graceful glider, the Mississippi kite summers in the southeastern and south-central United States. It feeds primarily on grasshoppers and dragonflies.*

RIGHT: *Poison ivy, seen here in a nineteenth-century book illustration, exudes an oily irritant that causes skin rashes. Its berrylike white seeds, however, provide winter food for a variety of birds.*

OVERLEAF: *Still, dark waters reflect bordering marsh grasses, flowering shrubs, and a variety of hardwoods at Big Hill Pond State Park near the Mississippi border.*

opened to the public as both an environmental education park and wildlife sanctuary.

Trails at the 65-acre nature center wind around a lake and through a pleasant woods of sweet gum, yellow poplar, sycamore, American elm, shagbark hickory, white oak, and red maple, many of them identified—as are eight types of ferns. The park offers marsh ecology and forest ecology teaching loops as well. Although buildings occasionally invade the view, dense foliage generally blots out thoughts of the city. A paved sensory trail provides those in wheelchairs or strollers access to sights and smells of the natural world, and all visitors can get close views of such Lichterman patients as injured red foxes, barred owls, or red-tailed hawks. The nature center is on Quince Avenue off Interstate 240. (And yes, Graceland is nearby, about 15 minutes to the west.)

EAST FROM MEMPHIS: ALONG THE BORDER AND BOARDWALKS

From Memphis, our loop through western Tennessee takes us 70 miles east along Route 57, just north of the Mississippi state line. At Pocahontas, in Tennessee's rolling red-clay area, is **Big Hill Pond State Park❖,** where a trail winding past the pond crosses Dismal Swamp on a boardwalk. The 4,218-acre park also has a lake, marsh, and pine and broadleaf forests.

Pl.167.

Rhus toxicodendron?

A network of minor roads in a pleasingly remote area north of Big Hill Pond goes about 40 miles north to **Chickasaw State Park❖,** located on Route 100 about 8 miles west of Henderson. The scenery along Route 100 is impressive: A mixed forest with towering pines flanks the highway, and stands of oaks, hickories, and pines border the park's Lake Placid. The lands were reclaimed by the Works Progress Administration and Civilian Conservation Corps in the 1930s, and although the park is highly developed with all manner of lodges, boat docks, archery ranges, and camp stores, birding experts report worthwhile outings, including several pleasant walking and riding trails that take about an hour each to travel.

ABOVE: *Vibrantly colored with white detailing, a male wood duck takes flight, exhibiting a long dark tail at one end and a long red bill at the other. Wood ducks nest in trees near calm waters, where snapping turtles often prey on the young ducks.*

RIGHT: *The deeply scaled, dark gray trunks of loblolly pines rise straight up on formerly depleted lands at Natchez Trace State Resort Park. The fragrant loblolly, known as the bull pine due to its size, grows nearly 100 feet tall.*

North and west of Chickasaw, near Brownsville, the Hatchie River flows across the northern border of **Hatchie National Wildlife Refuge❖** for 24 miles. This prime example of hardwood bottomland is home to otters and Swainson's warblers. About 15 miles of hiking and driving paths and roads wander through the quiet refuge.

About 30 miles east, in stark contrast to Hatchie River's wildness, **Cypress Grove Nature Park❖** sits just inside the western limits of Jackson on Route 70 west. The 165-acre park, operated by the city of Jackson, features a boardwalk that winds through a swamp and woodlands as highway traffic hums in the background. Sprinkled among the cypresses are eastern cottonwoods, American elms, black

willows, red maples, sweet gums, water tupelos, willow oaks, and hornbeams, many of which are identified along the boardwalk. The park's observation boxes and tower afford opportunities for the patient visitor to observe the languid takeoff of a blue heron or perhaps spot a white-tailed deer, turkey, mink, or raccoon.

JACKSON TO NASHVILLE: RECLAIMING THE LAND

Natchez Trace State Resort Park❖ and **Natchez Trace State Forest Resort**❖ are monuments both to humankind's rapacious past uses of land and current interests in righting the mistakes. Interstate 40 (Exit 116) intersects the park a few miles west of the Tennessee River, halfway between Nashville and Memphis. With 48,000 acres stretching more than 15 miles, Natchez Trace is the largest state forest in Tennessee. The Natchez Trace itself was a historic pioneer route between Nashville and Natchez, Mississippi; the park received its name because an offshoot of the trail ran through a section of its 14,000 acres.

Towering oaks and hickories, along with dogwoods, sassafras, and redbuds, once grew in the rich, sandy soil, but the forests were so heavily logged that much of the land was useless by the 1930s, a denuded wasteland of deep gullies. In 1935, under a New Deal program, 6,000 pine seedlings were planted in the initial efforts to restore the land. Today the park and forest are lush with tall pines, as well as cedars, oaks, hickories, and a dense understory dotted with wildflowers.

ABOVE: *Bloodroot, a member of the poppy family, thrives in fertile woods and along streams. Native Americans used red juice from its stem to dye cloth and baskets.*

RIGHT: *Glistening in the early morning light, spring trees brighten the shoreline of Maple Creek Lake in Natchez Trace State Park.*

OVERLEAF: *The Eagle Creek landscape glows in bands of orange, blue, and green at the Duck River Unit of the Tennessee wildlife refuge.*

One unfortunate but well-intentioned introduction was the Asian kudzu vine, a rapid grower that experts hoped would help arrest erosion. Its lengthy taproot, however, prevented that, and even worse, the plant grew as much as a foot per day, engulfing all in its path. The import turned out to be more of a suffocating enemy than a friend to the new forest, but, as the park's literature concludes, kudzu "is probably here to stay."

The park also harbors what is believed to be, at 106 feet, the third largest pecan tree in the world. Legend has it that the tree was planted by one of Andrew Jackson's soldiers en route home after the Battle of New Orleans. Legend or no legend, someone certainly planted it: Pecan trees are not native to this area.

The park and forest have more than 40 miles of trails that wind by lakes and through forests and open areas. Nearly 50 bird species have been sighted.

TENNESSEE RIVER/KENTUCKY LAKE

Nathan Bedford Forrest State Park❖, about 30 miles northeast of the Natchez Trace, is near the tiny town of Eva on Route 19 east of Camden. The park centers around Pilot Knob, at 665 feet the highest point on the western bank of the Tennessee River and a well-known landmark to riverboat pilots. General Nathan Bedford Forrest of the Confederate

Army destroyed a Union munitions and supply installation nearby in 1864. Accessible by car or a rigorous ten-mile hike on the Tennessee Forest Trail, Pilot Knob affords a panoramic view of what is now the Kentucky Lake section of the Tennessee River—plus factories and barges. The area is also known for its mussel industry, and exhibits explain the different types in the river/lake—washboard, pig toe, maple leaf, and pistol grip—as well as the development of cultivated pearls.

The park has 25 miles of long and short trails on both sides of the lake. Polk Creek Self-Guided Nature Trail, a gem for the less-energetic hiker, calls attention to examples of sycamore, muscadine vine, sweet gum, wild cherry, American beech, wild petunia, pink oxalis, blue flag iris, star-of-Bethlehem, bloodroot, yellow violet, and other species.

The National Wildlife Refuge system commenced when Theodore Roosevelt set aside Florida's Pelican Island in 1903. That initial effort saved the "millinery" birds—egret, heron, and other species whose feathers tickled the fashion fancies of turn-of-the-century ladies. The federal network has since grown to embrace more than 450 refuges, totaling more than 91 million acres, that protect species native to the United States.

ABOVE: *A blue-winged teal stretches its wing during a stopover in its migration over Tennessee; it is the first duck to head south in the fall and the last to fly north in the spring.*

LEFT: *With tenuous footholds, leafy hardwoods hug the rockbound shore of Ginger Bay in the Tennessee portion of Kentucky Lake.*

To the north of the state park, on a large promontory jutting into Kentucky Lake, sits the **Big Sandy Unit** of the **Tennessee National Wildlife Refuge❖,** a haven for ducks, geese, and other migratory birds. The wood duck, a tree nester, receives particular attention. Nesting boxes supplement the preserve's scarce natural tree cavities, and the refuge breeds several hundred wood ducks annually. The Big Sandy Unit is off Route 69A north of Big Sandy. The refuge has two other units to the south: Duck River on

193

ABOVE: *A meadow of perennial red clover stretches across flatlands in the Tennessee section of Land Between the Lakes, where the TVA*

the east bank of the lake, north of Interstate 40 near New Johnsonville; and Busselton off Route 69 along the western shore of the Tennessee River, northeast of Parsons.

Although the hand of man is inextricably prominent at **Land Between the Lakes❖,** in recent years the management of nature has been relatively benign here. Various aspects of the area have been described in superlatives—largest man-made this or that—and few would deny that the Tennessee Valley Authority's programs have benefited animals and plants as well as providing flood controls and recreational opportunities. For a full description of this huge area, see Chapter Four. From Tennessee, Land Between the Lakes is reached via Route 79 between Paris and Dover, three miles west of Fort Donelson National Battlefield.

ON THE CUMBERLAND

On the rambling, twisting Cumberland River east of Dover on Route 49 off Route 79, **Cross Creeks National Wildlife Refuge❖** was es-

maintains a mix of natural and managed areas. Introduced from Europe, this nitrogen-fixing plant is often used in crop rotation.

tablished in 1962, prompted by flooding that resulted from the damming to create Lake Barkley. The refuge, which is managed primarily for the benefit of migratory waterfowl, covers nearly 9,000 acres of varied terrain from wetlands and rich bottomlands to deciduous woodlands and rocky cliffs.

A key attraction is the bald eagle, a long-endangered, but now happily merely threatened, species that is represented here by a few permanent residents and a winter population of about a dozen birds. The first successful Tennessee nesting of this fish-feeding raptor in 22 years was achieved here in 1983. Other rare species observed at Cross Creeks include the Mississippi kite, wood stork, snow bunting, peregrine falcon, osprey, and golden eagle. More than 70 species are regarded as common or abundant.

The moisture level in the soil is managed by manipulating water levels of 16 impoundments and 2 reservoirs. The levels are drawn down in spring and summer to allow natural moist-soil vegetation to grow. Combined with agricultural crops grown by cooperative farmers, this

LEFT: *Among the many wildflowers at Cross Creeks, tubular red cardinal flowers (top) punctuate the wetter areas and white spider lilies (bottom) grow along the nature trails.*

RIGHT: *On a moist lake bank, a graceful American elm breaks out in spring foliage at the Cross Creeks National Wildlife Refuge.*

vegetation provides a variety of foods for migratory waterfowl. Sometimes 60,000 ducks visit during winter migrations, including the plentiful mallard, the finely decorated wood duck, and such diving species as canvasback, ringneck, bufflehead, and scaup. Migratory Canada geese sometimes exceed 50,000 in number.

More than 40 miles of roads and paths wind through forests of red oak, white oak, beech, sweet gum, black locust, cottonwood, willow, and redcedar. The woods are dotted with the delicate red cardinal flower, lush wild phlox, fire pink, and yellow Saint-John's-wort. Although primary consideration goes to migratory waterfowl, beavers, even with their dams removed, flourish along with eastern cottontails, fox squirrels and gray squirrels, striped skunks, and white-tailed deer.

WEST OF NASHVILLE: HIGHLAND RIM

From Cross Creeks, head south to the Highland Rim, the western edge of the Nashville Basin, to **Montgomery Bell State Resort Park❖** and its companion, **Harpeth Scenic River and Narrows Historic Area❖,** along Route 70 about 25 miles west of Nashville. Park trails edged with wildflowers wind by white oaks, rocky streams,

a spring that gushes 1,000 gallons of water per minute, and remnants of an iron furnace complex established by Montgomery Bell, who supplied cannonballs used by Andrew Jackson at the Battle of New Orleans in the War of 1812. A 100-yard tunnel cut through solid stone in 1819 for Bell's ironworks still attracts curious visitors.

Of prime interest in this area is a five-mile section of the Harpeth River. A canoeing party can embark at one point, travel five miles, and return to virtually the same spot without duplicating the route.

Immediately north of Harpeth, on Route 250, west of Route 49 out of Ashland City, is the 20,000-acre **Cheatham Wildlife Management**

197

Area❖, which is open to the public except during population-control hunts of deer and turkey. Old logging trails and a few new roads are open to hikers. One section of the beech-maple-white ash forest has been designated a natural area where no management is imposed.

NASHVILLE BASIN

At first **Bledsoe Creek State Park❖,** about 20 miles northeast of Nashville, seems to miss the mark as a significant natural site. Only 164 acres, it is heavily developed for camping, boating, swimming, and volleyball. Yet four miles of trails are tucked into this environmental education area, and even the gentle Birdsong, Wood Duck Cover Footpath conveys a sense of the wild as it moves through dense deciduous and redcedar woods with cattle grazing on the other side of a rock wall. Within a half hour, visitors may well spot pileated woodpeckers and white-tailed deer. Bledsoe is located on Old Hickory Lake off Route 25 about six miles east of Gallatin.

About 25 miles to the southeast, 8 miles south of Lebanon along Route 231, are another pair of companion sites, **Cedars of Lebanon State Park❖** and **Cedars of Lebanon State Forest❖,** both named for the biblical land. The largest redcedar forest in the United States grows here, the result of heavy reforesting after prolonged logging for the pencil industry. (In the 1920s only the straight heartwood was used to manufacture pencils, so about 75 percent of the wood was wasted.) The U.S. Department of

ABOVE: *Largest of the squirrel family, the fox squirrel comes in a variety of colors, including gray and yellow, bright orange, and—in the south—jet black.*

LEFT: *West of Nashville, eroded rock ledges, visible even below the water's turquoise surface, create a small, deep pool within the forest at Cheatham Wildlife Management Area.*

199

ABOVE: *With its young starting to explore the edges of their down-lined nest, a Canada goose watches for predators at Radnor Lake. Often grazing in farm fields, the ubiquitous Canada has become semidomesticated.*

Agriculture purchased area farmlands during the Great Depression, then hired the former owners to work there under the WPA; the first of 792,000 trees were planted in 1936. Although known as cedars, the trees are redcedars—no true cedars are native to the United States. Because the berry is quite hard, several techniques were developed to soften them enough to germinate—in natural circumstances, the shells are softened by acids in birds' digestive systems.

The park's limestone redcedar glades, which are found from Alabama north as far as Indiana, are a specific habitat for 19 wildflower species. The most endangered of the species found in Cedars of Lebanon is the Tennessee purple coneflower. Other plants include the highly aromatic glade mint, a glade lobelia, breadroot, and Gettinger's purple prairie clover. An aura of tranquillity pervades the eight miles of trails that wind through cedar glades, mossy rock outcroppings, limestone sinks, and caves. At some points the larger, gnarled trees evoke the harsh forms of a Léger painting.

The next stop takes us west toward metropolitan Nashville and **Long Hunter State Park❖,** which sprawls over 2,456 acres east of

ABOVE: *A female striped skunk and her young hunt for beetles, grasshoppers, and other insects around a decaying log. Ferociously protective, the mother will snarl, bare her teeth, and spray at intruders.*

the city off Route 171 between Interstates 24 and 40. The park features facilities for the handicapped: Its Couchville Lake Area is barrier free and has a paved, two-mile, self-guided nature trail. Several trails of varying difficulty are also provided.

Some 120 wildflower species include the Tennessee purple coneflower, Nashville breadroot, Missouri primrose, rose verbena, Guthrie's ground plum, limestone flame flower, sunnybell, glade larkspur, and leafy prairie clover. Cedar glades mark the flat and gently rolling lands around J. Percy Priest Lake, formed by the impoundment of Stones River. More than 60 species of birds flit among black willows, hickories, oaks, and maples. "Long Hunter" was a term often applied to early white explorers whose expeditions lasted a few months to a year or more; among them was Uriah Stone, for whom the Stones River was named.

NASHVILLE: A METROPOLITAN SANCTUARY

"The urban wildlife park in itself is somewhat of a paradoxical statement, an oxymoron," concedes Randy Vincent in a recent treatise on

Radnor Lake State Natural Area❖. Vincent is the naturalist at this metropolitan Nashville park and something of a poet on matters relating to nature. Despite its proximity to Nashville, however, Radnor is just the sort of jewel that justifies struggling with that inherent conflict between the real wild and the managed wild.

Radnor was created to serve the whims, not the essentials, of humankind, yet it quickly became a refuge for wildlife. Author Michael Lee Bierly has reported that "224 species of birds, 77 percent of the Nashville area list, have been recorded at Radnor."

Vincent can say, too, with deserved satisfaction, that "many people are surprised when they discover that large predators like the elusive bobcat and coyote are found, but not often seen" in Radnor's 1,000 acres at the city's southern limits, virtually in the shadow of Interstate 65 on Otter Creek Road off Route 31. The 85-acre Radnor Lake was impounded by the Louisville and Nashville Railroad Company in 1914, first to pro-

LEFT: *Not far from the bustle and bustle of the interstate and downtown Nashville, tranquil Radnor Lake is an urban oasis, supporting a wide variety of wildflowers, trees, and animals. Here sycamores, maples, willows, and an oak-hickory woodland grow along the rocky lakeshore.*

vide a water supply for its Radnor Railroad Yards and second to serve as a hunting and fishing site for L&N personnel. To the company's credit, it recognized quickly that the lake was coveted by various birds, so by 1923 the L&N banned hunting and fishing and declared the area a wildlife sanctuary. Eventually, in 1973, Tennessee's Department of Conservation acquired the land.

Vincent laments that "many urban wildlife parks are literally being loved to death." While the streams of hikers and lunch-hour strollers seen looping Radnor's little lake are not a menace individually, the numbers mount up to one million visitors annually.

With its strict controls, Radnor, however, remains a safe harbor for a vast number of aquatic and forest animal species and plant life. Guided canoe tours are among many supervised, scheduled events, but boating, fishing, hunting, swimming, and even jogging on the six miles of trails are prohibited.

An illustration of the changing natural environment is the recent proliferation, at Radnor and elsewhere in the Southeast, of the coyote. This close relative of the domestic dog has assumed part of the role of its large carnivore cousin, the red wolf, a species endangered in the wild and now bred under protection.

The Spillway Trail, Lake Trail, and South Lake Trail take the visitor roaming over some of the steepest territory in the Nashville Basin, the Overton Hills. Here many of the animals are nocturnal, but Vincent attests that "on any given day if park visitors will take the time to quietly walk around the lake or through the woodlands, they may be blessed with the glimpse of a barred owl or a great blue heron...." Within a 20-minute drive from the concrete, glass, and steel of state government buildings, Radnor provides a home to swallowtail butterflies, eastern chipmunks, whippoorwills, wood poppies, flowering dogwoods, and those lurking native bobcats.

ON AND OFF NATCHEZ TRACE

Southwest of Radnor Lake SNA, off Routes 100 and 96, is the northern access to the 445-mile **Natchez Trace Parkway❖** from Natchez, Mississippi, to Nashville. The parkway marks the trace, or route, used by the Natchez, Chickasaw, and Choctaw, as well as by French and Spanish explorers and settlers. (Ohio Valley settlers, for instance, floated their crops down the river to New Orleans and returned north on the trail.) By 1810 the trail was the most heavily traveled road in what was then called the Southwest.

Several sections of the old trace, with wayside exhibits interpreting its history, can still be seen and walked in Tennessee along this National Park System parkway. Highlights include short nature trails at mileposts 363 and 407.7, and the grave of western explorer Meriwether Lewis, of Lewis and Clark fame, at milepost 385.9. A national scenic trail has been designated within the parkway's boundaries, and more extensive hiking and horseback trails are planned.

For wonderful views and a sense of the past, follow the Natchez Trace Parkway south to milepost 370 and **Laurel Hill Wildlife Management Area❖** and **David Crockett State Park❖,** along Route 64 west of Lawrenceburg. The park honors Crockett because he once operated a gristmill and distillery along Shoal Creek and lived for six years in Lawrenceburg while serving in the state legislature. A reconstructed gristmill and museum exhibits elucidate the life of this famous frontiersman and member of Congress. The park is well equipped with amenities and recreations, but nature trails also wind through forests, and the bird-watching is good.

The line between what is natural and what is artificial becomes somewhat blurred when one considers the **Old Stone Fort Archaeological Area❖,** located about three miles southwest of Manchester on Route 41. High above a triangular pattern cut by the Duck River and the Little Duck River, Native Americans constructed an earthen-and-stone wall around a 50-acre plateau 2,000 years ago.

ABOVE: *Often waiting motionless to pounce on prey below, the wily bobcat mainly hunts rabbits, squirrels, and mice. Found only in North America, this common wildcat was named for its short, stubby tail.*

For many years, experts assumed the mound was built for defense; today conventional wisdom assigns an unspecified ceremonial function to it. Made of chert, limestone, and black shale, rocks for the mound were laboriously hauled from surrounding areas with neither horse nor wheel and then covered with earth. While there are few places in its mile-and-a-quarter circumference where it still approaches its original four- to six-foot height, most of the mound is clearly visible in a walk around the perimeter. At some places, the bluffs drop nearly 100 feet down to the river forks making their noisy way along terraces of rock. More than 80 wildflower species grow in the park. Among them are mountain laurel, yellow lady's slipper, jack-in-the-pulpit, white wood aster, woodland sunflower, and daisy fleabane. Some 40 bird species have been reported.

Pondering the mysteries of the past, we end our swing through Western-Middle Tennessee.

CHAPTER SIX

EASTERN TENNESSEE:
UP, DOWN, ALL AROUND

L ooking north over Chattanooga from Lookout Mountain on Tennessee's southern border, one immediately senses the relative flatness of the Cumberland Plateau, something that is difficult to perceive when traveling on it. From Chattanooga the plateau stretches south into Georgia and Alabama and extends west about 30 miles in Tennessee; northeast from Chattanooga, it arcs and widens across the state into southeastern Kentucky and across West Virginia (the Tennessee Valley sweeps south on the same axis). Below Lookout Mountain the Tennessee River dramatically meanders between the mountain and Moccasin Bend; to the east and northeast rise the Appalachian Mountains and their many ranges, including the Cumberlands.

That broad panorama makes Chattanooga an ideal starting point for the closing tour of this three-state Appalachian region. On the Cumberland Plateau the itinerary goes to Prentice Cooper State Forest at Signal Mountain and then, heading north, takes in the forests, waterfalls, lakes, and geological features of the South Cumberland Recreation Area. Administered by Tennessee State Parks, South Cumberland radiates from Tracy City, encompassing sites with such inviting names as Grundy Forest, Stone Door, and Savage Gulf, and a trail called Fiery Gizzard.

LEFT: *In June, thousands of visitors—local residents and travelers alike—trek to see the spectacular catawba rhododendrons in full bloom atop Roan Mountain on the Tennessee–North Carolina border.*

All of these places (except for Prentice Cooper) are west of the 70-mile-long Sequatchie Valley, which is bordered on its east by Walden Ridge. East of the ridge lies the Tennessee Valley, a continuation of West Virginia's Shenandoah Valley. Sometimes called the Great Valley of East Tennessee, it is about 50 miles wide and has its own ridges and hills. All of these features are subdivisions of the Cumberland Plateau.

Next, the route proceeds to Fall Creek Falls, one of the tallest waterfalls in the East, followed by a series of caves and, near Cookeville and Crossville, more waterfalls, including some that disappear into the ground. To the east around Wartburg is some primitive backcountry surrounding the Obed River, which is primarily known for its white water, and Frozen Head Mountain, which—despite its forbidding name—beckons wildflower enthusiasts.

From there the itinerary heads north to the Kentucky border and Big South Fork National River and Recreation Area, which encompasses a major tributary of the Cumberland River and features numerous gorges, waterfalls, and natural arches. Then, after a few more stops, the route leaves the Cumberland Plateau and crosses Clinch Mountain in the Appalachian ridge-and-valley province, heading south to the Blue Ridge and its many ranges. Here the Cherokee National Forest and Great Smoky Mountains National Park are splendid showcases for more than 1,400 plant species that prosper in Tennessee, along with a wide variety of mammals, reptiles, fish, and birds.

Having described this tour in broad terms, it is time once again to remind you to get out of the car, stretch your legs, and take a closer look at the smaller things. "The rays of the early morning sun bombard the tops of the trees above the headwaters of Forney Creek," Napier Shelton writes in *The Great Smoky Mountains*. "Some penetrate the canopy to make light patches in the lower layers of the forest. But few break through the rhododendron thickets along the stream to illuminate its mossy rocks, its foam, and its clear pools. Down in the darkness beneath overhanging shrubs, hanging in the current near the bottom of a pool, a brook trout waits for the stream to bring it food. With dark mottling along its back, red spots on its olive sides, and pale orange edging on its lower fins, the fish is beautiful."

Such scenes await not only in the big places but in the small ones as well. As Annie Dillard, in her essay "Seeing," says: "There are lots

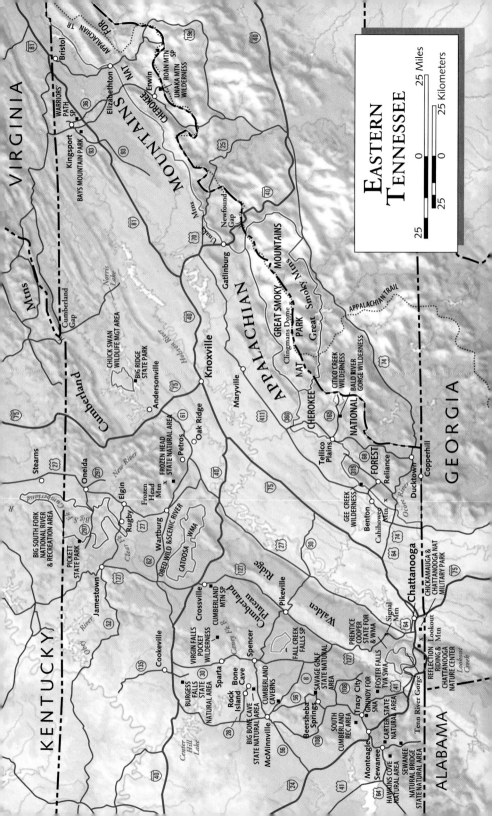

ABOVE: *On a rock shelf, a cluster of bright pink redbud blossoms artistically occupies a narrow crevice between moss- and lichen-covered sandstone boulders at the Sewanee Natural Bridge State Natural Area.*

of things to see, unwrapped gifts and free surprises." This tour begins with one of those surprises, at the foot of Lookout Mountain.

CHATTANOOGA: ON REFLECTION

Chattanooga has a number of attractions memorable for their natural origins, but several of them show a heavy entrepreneurial hand. A welcome respite from the commercialism is provided by **Reflection Riding and Chattanooga Nature Center❖** between the western slopes of Lookout Mountain and Lookout Creek off Route 41. A 300-acre botanical garden and nature study facility, Reflection Riding supports more than 1,000 varieties of shrubs, flowers, and trees. The many labeled species include red maple, water oak, American beech, swamp dogwood, slippery elm, arrowwood, red chokeberry, the yaupon shrub, bamboo, and oakleaf hydrangea.

Besides exhibits and the many programs put on for metropolitan schoolchildren by the nature center, one of the key educational attractions is a 1,200-foot wetlands walk through a marsh, wet meadows,

ABOVE: *In a crevice on another rock shelf, a bright orange cave sala-mander forages for insects. Found in Tennessee, Kentucky, and parts of West Virginia, this salamander frequents only limestone areas.*

wooded swamps, and bottomland forests (which can be flooded on occasion). This raised boardwalk is designed for wheelchair users as well as hikers. The three-mile auto "riding" tour through the grounds alludes to the quaint English definition of a riding path as a path of pleasure, and a pleasure it is to ride or walk by and through such a variety of plant life in meadows, woodlands, ponds, and creeks. Radiating from various points along the primitive road, 12 miles of trails connect with similar trails in the adjacent 2,700-acre **Lookout Mountain and Point Park Unit** of the **Chickamauga and Chattanooga National Military Park❖** that commemorates a hard-fought Civil War battle. From the mountain, the views of the plateau are spectacular.

Heading northwest from Chattanooga on Route 27 and then Route 127 north, stunningly beautiful **Signal Mountain**—a part of Walden Ridge—looms up on the west as the highway climbs abruptly. Only ten miles beyond Chattanooga lies **Prentice Cooper State Forest and Wildlife Management Area❖,** which covers 26,000 acres of woodlands. Three miles into the park, hikers can access a ten-mile section of

the **Cumberland Trail** that eventually links up with other sections until it reaches the Cumberland Gap, 200 miles farther along the plateau to the northeast. At Prentice Cooper the trail offers fine views of the Tennessee River Gorge, a 1,200-foot-deep canyon slicing through Walden Ridge. The gorge is the fourth largest east of the Mississippi. According to Russ Manning in *The Historic Cumberland Plateau,* some 1,000 varieties of plants can be found in the area, including such rare or endangered species as mountain skullcap, rose gentian, and mountain mint.

SOUTH CUMBERLAND'S VARIED CHARMS

The remarkable and far-flung **South Cumberland Recreation Area❖** consists of several natural features and sites spread over a 100-square-mile area. The main visitor center serving this network is on Route 56 between Tracy City and Monteagle about 30 miles northwest of Chattanooga, and it is wise to go there first to get a good understanding of the whole area and its many parts. For logistical purposes, this route will trace South Cumberland's charms from its southwest corner to the north and east.

The 250-acre **Hawkins Cove Natural Area❖** was established in 1985 primarily to preserve the Cumberland rosinweed, a rare species. Hawkins Cove is on Route 64 about ten miles west of the visitor center and five miles west of the town of Sewanee. South of Sewanee on Route 56 are **Carter State Natural Area❖** and **Sewanee Natural Bridge State Natural Area❖.** The two-mile Buggytop Trail at Carter leads to Lost Cove Cave, inhabited

ABOVE: *The belted kingfisher, shown in an 1808 pastel by John James Audubon, will dive from a branch, catching fish with its bill, or hover over water, plunging in headfirst.*

LEFT: *At 100 feet wide and 80 feet high, Lost Cove Cave opens under a bluff at Carter State Natural Area, one of many delights within the South Cumberland Recreation Area.*

OVERLEAF: *Sewanee Natural Bridge, a sandstone arch, stands 27 feet high and extends for 50 feet. The 1.5-acre site was donated to the state of Tennessee by the University of the South.*

213

by the Tennessee cave salamander and big-eared bat. Sewanee Natural Bridge is a sandstone arch standing 27 feet high. East of Interstate 24, along Route 41, **Foster Falls TVA Small Wild Area❖** boasts a 60-foot-high waterfall.

North of the falls and south of Tracy City on Route 41 are **Grundy Forest State Natural Area❖** and **Grundy Lakes State Park❖**, a swimming and picnic facility. In the late nineteenth century, coal was

mined and turned into coke in this area using convict labor, and a few coke ovens remain on the grounds. With 212 acres, Grundy Forest provides the northern access to Fiery Gizzard Trail, which takes its name from a yarn about Davy Crockett burning himself in the course of a campfire turkey dinner. The trail, one of South Cumberland's treasures, stretches 12 miles south to Foster Falls. In *Tennessee Trails,* Evan Means describes portions of it as "exceptionally spectacular, but very difficult. The huge trees, rock formations, waterfalls, and cool swimming holes are well worth the struggle over the millions of rocks." The terrain varies dramatically, descending rapidly toward Fiery Gizzard Creek as the route heads south, then ascending again after following

ABOVE: *The wild columbine graces woodlands and slopes with its delicate bell-like flowers.*

the creek, with its many waterfalls and cascades, for several miles. One section passes hemlocks thought to be at least 400 years old. A two-mile loop near the Grundy Forest picnic area provides a good introduction to the countryside's variety.

North of Grundy Forest, Route 41 intersects at Tracy City with Route 56, which leads north to **Stone Door** at Beersheba Springs, and to **Savage Gulf State Natural Area❖.** A short trail leads to a giant crevice in a bluff at an elevation of about 1,800 feet. About 10 feet wide and 100 feet deep, the opening, or Stone Door, provided an interior passage for the Chickamauga to descend from the escarpment's top.

Stone Door is near the western boundary of the Savage Gulf. In this part of the country, deep canyons are traditionally referred to as gulfs, and this one is named for Samuel Savage, an early settler. Covering more than 11,500 acres, 95 percent of the South Cumberland Recreation Area, the Savage Gulf area is traversed by 13 trails totaling 55 miles. Several streams flow underground, except in particularly wet weather when they appear aboveground. Some rivers disappear over waterfalls that pour into sinkholes. A 500-acre virgin forest brims with maple, hickory, yellow poplar, ash, beech, and hemlock.

One third of the 2,120 plant species known to grow in Tennessee are found within the South Cumberland's four ecological zones: plateau top, bluff, gulf, and aquatic. The cool temperatures at Savage Gulf support various species more generally associated with areas well to the north of Tennessee; false hellebore, for example, is believed to grow only here. To protect delicate plant species, one deeply descending path is restricted to ranger-led expeditions.

ABOVE: *Not to be outshone, shooting star, or prairie pointer, puts on a fine spring show.*

For the most part ecological managers at South Cumberland try to leave nature alone no matter how tempting and positive intervention might seem. Their philosophy holds that protecting one species rather than another puts humanity in the place of a predator, disturbing normal population patterns. Rangers even refrain from spraying against the Tennessee pine beetle, which eats the cambium of trees and thus kills them. This hands-off strategy is also behind the decision not to create the less-brushy understory preferred

OVERLEAF: *In Fall Creek Falls State Resort Park, the setting sun glances off high bluffs and table mountain pines, providing a golden counterpoint to the green woodlands of the surrounding Cumberland Plateau.*

by the red-cockaded woodpecker. This species was believed to have disappeared from this area in the 1920s, and its existence is again threatened. One exception to the policy is a short hunting season to control the number of deer, which have no natural predator in the region since the disappearance of cougars.

ABOVE: *Clusters of closed, or bottle, gentians punctuate fallen leaves along Byrd Lake at Cumberland Mountain State Rustic Park.*

RIGHT: *A pink redbud and white Japanese deutzia in Rock Island State Park bloom beside the cascading Caney Fork River.*

PIKEVILLE TO COOKEVILLE: FALLS, CAVES, BONES, AND BATS

The tallest waterfall in the eastern United States is the namesake of **Fall Creek Falls State Resort Park❖,** approached via Route 111 or Route 30 about 11 miles east of Spencer and 18 miles west of Pikeville. Fall Creek twists through high ground at 1,800 feet in elevation, approaches a dramatic eroded gorge, and then plunges 256 feet into a copper-colored basin. Though its plunge is greater than Niagara's, the volume of water is not large, allowing visitors to play in the stream of water below. Old-growth hemlocks and yellow poplars (or tulip trees) line the exposed layers of the gorge. A strenuous trail does wind down to the falls itself, but appreciation for its height is more readily achieved from the overlook.

The park is highly developed for recreation on its dam-created lake, but about 10,000 of its 15,000 land acres have been designated a state natural area. Thirty miles of trails of varying difficulty wander through the park and provide opportunities to see other major waterfalls, gurgling cascades, and steep gulfs, or gorges. The competition for attention is fierce. At one point, a plaque writer waxed eloquent: "Like a ribbon of silver streaming through a green velvet pillow, Piney Creek Falls cascades 75 feet into a rugged, lush gorge. . . . Powerful and remote, Piney Creek Falls is the park's most beautiful to many visitors." Nearby a pine grows around and above a heavy flat rock, creating the im-

RIGHT: *In the second act of a flowing three-act play, Middle Falls tumbles over rocky ledges into a pool of swirling waters dotted with tiny islands. The Obey River then races on to its grand finale at Burgess Falls, which has given its name to this park.*

pression of a natural picnic table.

Ambitious hikers can take two loops that total 25 miles along forests and fern beds on the plateau, passing three waterfalls on the way into Cane Creek Gorge. Oaks and hickories cover most of the park except in the moist gorges, where forests of hemlocks and yellow poplars are home to other plants and animals similar to those that thrive in southern Canada. Rhododendrons and mountain laurels are sprinkled throughout the park.

A concentration of erodible limestone in the earth's underlying layers accounts in part for the presence of numerous caverns west of Fall Creek Falls. Caves, with their sense of mystery, their dark, dank coolness, their elegant rock formations, and their deceptive sense of changelessness, have long lured humans. Unfortunately, many of the caverns in this region tend to be either highly developed as tourist attractions or too delicate or dangerous to be freely available for public use. Clustered near McMinnville, about 20 miles west along Route 30, are several examples of each.

The most accessible is the vast **Cumberland Caverns❖,** on Route 8 about seven miles southeast of McMinnville. Reputed to rank second only to Mammoth Cave in the length of its underground passageways, highly developed Cumberland Caverns even has a 500-seat dining room (open by prearrangement only). Its natural Hall of the Mountain King, a vast chamber that measures 600 feet long, 150 feet wide, and 140 feet high, is possibly the largest individual cave room east of the Mississippi.

Bones of a giant sloth from the Pleistocene epoch were discovered in 1811 in **Big Bone Cave❖,** and saltpeter for ammunition was mined there during the War of 1812 and the Civil War. The cave still contains

well-preserved saltpeter vats. Near the town of Bone Cave about 15 miles northeast of McMinnville, the cave is now a state natural area and is accessible only through tours prearranged with **Rock Island State Park❖,** a recreation area on Route 287 west of the towns of Rock Island and Bone Cave.

Also available solely by prior arrangement, **Hubbard's Cave❖** is only for experienced cave explorers. Located southeast of McMinnville, along the Collins River, Hubbard's Cave houses Tennessee's largest concentration of hibernating gray myotis, an endangered species of bat.

Where the Falling Water River section of the Obey River hurries toward Center Hill Lake, the coursing current takes three distinct

223

plunges of increasing size, climaxing at Burgess Falls. The whole sequence is the raison d'être for the **Burgess Falls State Natural Area❖,** on Route 135 about 8 miles south of Interstate 40 north of Sparta and south of Cookeville. The series of falls is easily viewed from a winding, somewhat difficult path that traces the river. All along, smaller streams and lesser falls descend to join the gathering river, their gentle flows in stark contrast to the swirling surge below.

The modest Little Falls is near park headquarters. About a half mile farther along is Middle Falls, which splays around small green islands, its foamy, curved steps arranged like a wedding cake. Another quarter mile away, Burgess Falls plunges over an outcropping almost as pointed as an arrowhead. Below, water has curved the cliffs into a graceful bowl shape. In late spring and summer afternoons arcs of a rainbow sometimes seem to rise out of the pool at the bottom of the falls. Migrating osprey have been sighted in the park.

East of Burgess Falls lies **Virgin Falls Pocket Wilderness❖,** where streams wind through second-growth hardwoods on the edge of the Cumberland Plateau, make a splash, and disappear. The area is managed as part of the Bowater Paper Company's natural area program. The entrance is six miles south of Route 70 between Sparta and Crossville. Look for a Pocket Wilderness sign between Bon Air and De Rossert. Virgin Falls presents a particularly mysterious and stunning visual reward to intrepid hikers.

At the falls, a creek emerges suddenly from the ground, runs no more than 50 feet, and then plunges 110 feet over a precipice. Below, it disappears again, running into rock caves at the bottom. Another creek runs out of Sheep Cave and cascades some 60 feet before it disappears into a hole, and Big Laurel Falls plunges into a cave. The show is like a three-act play, and behind the scenes these underground flows probably drain into Caney Fork River. Hiking from the parking area to Virgin Falls and back takes six to eight hours, plenty of time to enjoy the area's many wildflowers along the way.

Cumberland Mountain State Rustic Park❖ is quite a contrast to remote Virgin Falls. Although it has a well-developed park with lodge, restaurant, and cabins, the area is also wild enough to be a favorite among birders who appreciate its cool climate and wooded terrain. The 1,562-acre park is four miles south of Crossville along Route 127 and only about ten minutes from Interstate 40. Six trails ramble over 15 miles. The five-mile Pioneer Loop winds through a hemlock forest, and even the one-mile Cumberland Plateau Trail, starting near the lodge, offers an immediate respite. After a June rain, the trail's rhododendron leaves shimmer among the last of the spring blossoms, and lichens nestling between large bark segments of shortleaf pine glow with a greenish iridescence. Some 36 bird species have been spotted here, including the yellow-billed cuckoo, red-eyed vireo, belted kingfisher, rufous-sided towhee, and Carolina chickadee.

FROM OBED TO FROZEN HEAD

During wet winters and in the spring, kayaking, rafting, and canoeing enthusiasts from around the world head for the **Obed Wild and Scenic River❖,** 45 miles of rushing river and swirling stream. The waters were federally designated as part of the Wild and Scenic River system in 1976. The designation recognizes stretches as wild or scenic depending on development along the banks. The 45-mile length is only about half of what various conservation groups sought to protect. The National Park Service tries to protect the area and, in a delicate balance between beauty and commerce, recognizes that the private tracts along the river might not be used in accordance with conservationists' aims. Easements have been purchased when possible.

During the summer, the Obed hardly seems wild as it moves slowly amid boulders, but it is deliciously remote. Families with small children can drive to one of the infrequent boating accesses and wade in water barely a foot deep. Of course, swimmers must be careful during times of heavy rain, when the river may rise suddenly. High above, steep bluffs bespeak the territory's ruggedness and offer some assurance that nature will continue to triumph over human capriciousness here.

Obed's visitor center is on Route 27 in Wartburg, and access points to the river begin about five miles to the west off Route 62. The park actually includes Daddy's Creek, Clear Creek, and Emory River as well as parts of the Obed proper. These rivers have sliced 500-foot gorges into the surrounding Cumberland Plateau, which is clothed with forests of pine, maple, hickory, and hemlock, along with luxurious rhododendron, azalea, and mountain laurel. Some 100 species of birds live in the region, and animals such as mink, fox, and bobcat relish the ruggedness of the

land, which has long made it virtually impossible to farm or inhabit.

"It is one of the few remaining places in the country where waters run free and there has been little or no change in the natural sequence of events," Park Service literature asserts. Fortunately, various surveys concluded that it would be impractical to dam the Obed for recreational purposes, and Congress gave its official blessing to leave the river alone. White-water rafting is dangerous when the Obed runs with full veins, and even hikers are urged to have a companion at all times, because there are no developed facilities or formal trails. Be sure to stop at the visitor center before heading into this primitive backcountry.

Portions of the Obed complex run through the **Catoosa Wildlife Management Area❖,** at nearly 80,000 acres the largest area managed by the Tennessee Wildlife Resources Agency. The area stretches south of Route 62 and east of Route 127/28. At Catoosa deer, wild turkeys, ruffed grouse, and bobcats roam naturally through hardwood and pine forests at about 2,000 feet of elevation. Russian wild boars

ABOVE: *With screams, chitters, and grunts, a bald eagle calls to its mate; the giant raptors are gradually returning to parts of the Catoosa Wildlife Management Area.*

LEFT: *When water levels decrease in the autumn, huge boulders appear along the rocky Obed River near Clear Creek—a stark contrast to the rushing spring torrents that thrill expert kayakers.*

were brought to the area in the early 1900s and, having few predators, prospered. Today they are rarely seen, but they upturn plenty of earth.

The endangered Cumberland Plateau musky is among the species of fish native to the area, along with catfish, redeye, and bass. Except during hunting season, birding is excellent, with species such as infrequently spotted golden eagles, threatened bald eagles, and red-cockaded woodpeckers. Old logging roads make for good hiking except during several winter months, when Catoosa is closed to recover from the hunting season.

Early in the nineteenth century, settlers from the highlands of

ABOVE: *Living solely in old-growth pine forests, a now-rare red-cockaded woodpecker works on a hole high in the canopy.*

RIGHT: *A meadow of white valerian, an herb known as corn-salad or lamb's lettuce, flourishes in the Big South Fork National River and Recreation Area.*

Wales and Scotland found certain familiar aspects in the Cumberland Mountains. At **Frozen Head State Natural Area❖**, spanning 11,869 acres five miles east of Wartburg, the lofty, rugged terrain still illustrates those similarities, providing many a stunning view for those who endure the harsh hiking. The natural area includes 14 mountain peaks with elevations more than 3,000 feet, and at 3,324 feet, the area's namesake, Frozen Head Mountain. The lowest point is 1,340 feet, and the great changes in elevation provide habitat for 120 species of wildflowers, making **Frozen Head Mountain** second in the region to the Great Smokies for flowering displays. During spring, guided tours are given by experts. The mountain's name alludes to the high peaks' tendency to remain frozen while the lower valleys are snowless. Surface-mining in the nearby area has been restricted because it would detract from views within the park.

Twenty hiking trails meander for some 50 miles to giant rock houses, caprocks, and boulders, and several of them entail dramatic climbs amid steep cliffs. For example, the 7-mile North Bird Mountain Trail undergoes elevation gains and losses that total more than 6,000 feet; Chimney Top Trail covers 6.6 miles and undergoes 3,460 feet of elevation change.

CUMBERLAND'S BIG SOUTH FORK

A critical issue facing most scenic natural areas is just how accessible and popular

they can be before usage undermines their purpose of preserving wild lands. Such concerns, happily, can seem distant indeed when one stands in total isolation atop Honey Creek Overlook in the midst of **Big South Fork National River and Recreation Area❖.** Some 600 feet below, the Big South Fork of the Cumberland River runs clockwise around a bend as vast forested areas compete with rugged rock outcroppings for a viewer's attention. The erosion of sandstone over millennia created this sylvan haven, and some 60 years of natural orchestration has helped restore it to wilderness after decades of logging.

Straddling the Kentucky border, this recreation area covers more than 110,000 acres and was subject to various public, commercial, and legislative ambitions before being developed—but not dammed—by the U.S. Army Corps of Engineers. It was then turned over to the National Park Service, which gradually began to take over administration of the area in 1976, acquiring complete responsibility in 1990.

Big South Fork's main entrance is on Route 297 about nine miles west of Oneida, and the contour of the roadway demonstrates the dramatic erosion of the Cumberland Plateau as the route spirals quickly downward, then whirls back upward just as sharply after crossing Big South Fork south of Angel Falls. Another entrance option is to sample the intoxicating remoteness provided by swinging west from Elgin onto Route 52, past the remains of the short-lived experimental utopian village of Rugby, founded by British author-reformer Thomas Hughes in the 1880s. Continue northward into the park on Mount Helen Road to Honey Creek. (The second route touches just a portion of the recreation area and commits one to a circuitous route to Oneida, so look at a map before taking that option.)

The Big South Fork of the Cumberland River and its various tributaries provide plenty of opportunities for rafting, canoeing, and kayaking enthusiasts to test their skills—the full gamut from the thrills of white water to the lazy joys of a gentle paddle through a scenic natural landscape dotted with relics of abandoned settlements.

LEFT: *Massive ridges and cliffs tower over the Big South Fork of the Cumberland River, which has cut deep into the Cumberland Plateau.*
OVERLEAF: *Shared by Tennessee and Kentucky, Big South Fork includes Devil's Jump, site of awesome and hazardous springtime rapids.*

LEFT: *A good climber, the gray fox often rests on tree limbs but usually dens down below in hollow trunks or rocky ridges.*
RIGHT: *A black bear sow takes her two off spring on an educational feeding expedition. Cubs customarily stay with their protective mothers for at least 18 months.*

Here the New River and the Clear Fork join to form the Big South Fork, the third largest tributary of the Cumberland River, which winds through Tennessee and eventually heads north into Kentucky. The Big South Fork has cut deep into the lower sandstone layers of the Cumberland Plateau, and elevations rise from 800 feet along the river to 1,800 feet along the highest ridges. From the top, the plateau's flatness becomes quickly evident—the elevation of adjoining ridges is rather uniform.

Although the waterways are a magnet to recreationists, the park offers a wide assortment of natural arches, rock shelters, waterfalls, and bluffs. New forests cover most of the logged-over and mined lands, and colorful wildflowers brighten the shores of the waterways with blooms starting in early March and continuing into the fall. The best trails to see wildflowers in the Tennessee portion are the Angel Falls and Leatherwood Ford boardwalks and Gentleman's Swimming Hole, and in the Kentucky portion, Blue Heron Loop, Catawba Overlook, and Yahoo Falls.

Trails lead to interesting natural features such as Twin Arches, a pair of towering stone arches that ranks among the highest on the plateau at 51 and 70 feet and also longest, at 93 and 135 feet. Altogether, there are more than 150 miles of hiking trails ranging from a mile to more than 50 miles long, and more than 130 miles of blazed horse trails. Be warned. The trails down into the deep gorges are strenuous.

Among endangered plant species that grow in the recreation area are Virginia spiraea, Lucy Braun snakeroot, and Cumberland rosewood. Among wildlife, three nationally endangered species have been spotted here: peregrine falcon, red-cockaded woodpecker, and

234

Indiana myotis. The threatened bald eagle has been seen here as well; representing endangered fish is the spotfin chub. It is good bird-watching country with more than 200 inhabitant and migratory bird species. And black bears might be sighted, for the National Park Service is in the process of reintroducing them in the area.

The Kentucky section of Big South Fork is surrounded by Daniel Boone National Forest and is reachable from Stearns, Kentucky, north of Oneida. From April through October a train, with interpretative narration, runs 8 miles from Stearns to Blue Heron, an old Kentucky mining community in a deep gorge within the recreation area. The 254-mile **Sheltowee Trace National Recreation Trail❖** (see Chapter Three) crosses the park's northern panhandle, reentering the wilderness area again before it terminates in Pickett State Park. A section of the **John Muir Trail❖** also runs through the recreation area to the state park. This trail, named for the founder of the Sierra Club, will eventually be extended to follow Muir's 1867 1,000-mile route through Tennessee.

Pickett State Park❖, which is bordered by Big South Fork on the east and Kentucky on the north, encompasses 11,700 acres in the upper Cumberland Mountains northeast of Jamestown. Enormous rock formations lead to terraces where visitors can sit and ponder the

Above: *In a surge of white spray, the Tellico River cascades over rocky ledges carpeted with velvety green mosses and newly fallen autumn leaves at Bald River Falls in Tennessee's Cherokee National Forest.*

size and age of the mountains. Nearly 50 miles of trails pass through forests and gorges and by caves, waterfalls, and sandstone natural bridges. Although Pickett is known as the state's wilderness park, it has several short trails for the nonbackpacker constructed by the Civilian Conservation Corps in the 1930s, and some unmarked roadways maintained for management and logging purposes provide enticing avenues for hikers to enjoy the dense woods in relative privacy.

LAKES NEAR URBAN AREAS

Norris Lake, about 11 miles north of Knoxville, was the first lake created by the Tennessee Valley Authority after the agency was founded in 1933. Norris Dam was credited with preventing a flood along the Mississippi River four years later when it impounded streams and rivers that otherwise would have exacerbated rising waters hundreds of miles to the west. The formation of Norris Lake was followed by the establishment of "demonstration" parks in the area where the TVA hoped to show how recreational and quasi-natural facilities could successfully coexist.

One demonstration park is 3,687-acre **Big Ridge State Park❖** off Route 61 about eight miles north of Andersonville. Big Ridge and the neighboring **Chuck Swann Wildlife Management Area❖** (accessible by boat or via Route 33) stretch along the shorelines of Norris Lake. Some of the 15 miles of trails trace the park's namesake, Big Ridge, 1,500 feet in elevation. Bird-watching is fine in the Norris Lake area, and delicate pink lady's slippers bloom along Big Valley Trail. White-tailed deer have been known to graze nonchalantly in a meadow of tall grass only 30 yards from a busy tennis court. Although the park has clusters of cabins, campsites, and sports facilities and surrounding Anderson County seems bent on development, the quiet lake and the peaceful pine and hardwood forests radiate a superb serenity on summer mornings.

In the northeast corner of the state near Kingsport are two small parks. **Warriors' Path State Park❖,** three miles north of Interstate 81 on Hemlock Road off Route 36, surrounds Patrick Henry Reservoir on the Holston River. The 1,000-acre park is named for its proximity to an old route used by the Cherokee. Among the ten miles of trails, Devil's Backbone provides views of the river and the reservoir as it winds uphill and downhill through hardwoods and ends at Fall Creek, where carp and other fish bask in shadows along the banks. Deer are bountiful, and mink have been seen.

Across Route 36, take Moreland Drive, then Route 93 south and follow signs for **Bays Mountain Park❖,** on Route 137. This park, owned by the city of Kingsport, gets its name from its 44-acre mountaintop lake. With 3,000 acres and some 25 miles of hiking trails, Bays Mountain is an excellent spot for bird-watching and also has a nature center and planetarium.

CHEROKEE NATIONAL FOREST—NORTH

This book began in the Appalachian Mountains in West Virginia's Blue Ridge and Alleghenies. Now it appropriately closes with a swing south through the Appalachians along Tennessee's eastern border with North Carolina. All but a fraction of these mountainous lands are

OVERLEAF: *Thick, lush, vivid, plush—the adjectives keep flowing when one views the native catawba rhododendron on Roan Mountain, thought to hold the world's largest natural collection of this shrub.*

within a vast national forest and a large national park that divides the forest in two. **Cherokee National Forest❖** sprawls over nearly 630,000 acres in ten counties, from Bristol in the north to just outside Chattanooga in the south, and follows the northeast to southwest axis of the Unaka–Great Smoky Mountains chain. The only national forest in Tennessee, it abuts other large national forests in Virginia, North Carolina, and Georgia.

Compounding that complexity, Cherokee National Forest has within it several titled scenic areas and wilderness areas, nine major rivers, a scenic byway, and six ranger districts. Many highways and country roads wind up and down and through the various public lands and communities, connecting the various entities. More than 500 miles of trails are provided for hiking, along with more than 100 miles intended primarily for horseback riding and 80 miles for motorcycles, mountain bikes, and bicycles. In addition, that wonderful 2,144-mile hiking route from Maine to Georgia, the **Appalachian National Scenic Trail❖,** enters northern Tennessee in the national forest, crosses Roan Mountain, and for the most part follows the state's eastern border before exiting south after a 70-mile crest-line stretch in Great Smoky Mountains National Park.

Be sure to pick up maps of the national forest not only to identify trails but also to discover secondary and primitive road details. It is easy to wind down the other side of a mountain and find yourself miles away from where you want to be.

Elevations within the forest range from 800 to 6,285 feet, and many peaks are higher than 5,000 feet. Like the Smokies to the southwest, most of the lands were heavily logged, so most of the forests are second-growth hardwoods with spruce, fir, and some pines. About 135 fish species, including several that are endangered or threatened, inhabit the streams and rivers; about 50 types of mammals and more than 120 bird species occupy the woods and meadows.

About 15 miles south of Elizabethton on Route 143 off Route 19E **Roan Mountain State Park❖** boasts outstanding rhododendron

---

RIGHT: *Among the more than 1,400 flowering plant species found in Great Smoky Mountains National Park are (clockwise from top left) bright red fire pink; white and lavender showy orchis; and blue crested dwarf iris growing with white-flowered stonecrop, a succulent herb.*

Above: *Fraser's sedge is uncommon except in the Great Smoky Mountains, where it grows in rich woodlands and along streams. Unlike most sedges, it has many leaves and flowers and blooms in April and May.*

areas. (Visitors often mistake the 600-acre Rhododendron Gardens atop Roan Mountain for part of the park, but the gardens actually are on **Pisgah National Forest** lands, just over the North Carolina border.) Such designations seem not to matter on a foggy summer morning, when the clouds waft over and around Roan High Bluff, perhaps explaining why one of the trails is known as Cloudlands, as was a turn-of-the-century hotel. Here in June, at 6,285 feet of elevation, the catawba rhododendron blooms spatter the ridges with their great balls of succulent reddish purple, pink, and lavender. Ferns, grasses, swaths of buttercups, and an occasional blue violet further brighten the scene. Nearby, evergreen stands soldier on, the spruce scraggly from cold, snowy winters and short growing seasons, the Fraser firs weakened and dying from infestations of the balsam woolly adelgid.

Several grass balds and shrub, or heath, balds are nearby. Although bereft of trees, these steeply rounded hills are lush with wavy, knee-high grasses, wildflowers, rhododendrons, delicate heather, and other plants. Scientists have struggled to explain how these areas were denuded of woods—suggesting over-pasturing, severe weather, acidity, or fires as the cause—but have not come up with a definitive answer. Visitors can absorb the balds' compelling melancholy and simple beauty northwest of Carver's Gap, also a wonderful place to watch migrating raptors.

The source of the name Roan Mountain has many explanations as well. Perhaps the name springs from the roan color of the mountainsides awash in rhododendrons, or the story that Daniel Boone visited the area on a roan horse, or the numerous mountain ash trees also known as rowans that grow here. No one knows the answer.

Covering 2,156 acres, the state park has 8 hiking trails winding 17 miles through forests that change rapidly with their elevations. Areas below 3,500 feet are dominated by oak forests that give way to beech-maple and then, above 5,000 feet, to spruce-fir forests. Because its vegetation resembles the far north, the spruce-fir forests often are called the Canadian zone. The metamorphic gneiss and igneous granite that make up the mountain may be up to one billion years old. More than 180 wildflower species and 150 bird species are found in Roan Mountain forests. Along with white-tailed deer, bobcats, and foxes, some black bears have been reported.

THE UNAKAS

Some 20 miles west and slightly south of Roan Mountain is the town of Erwin, where, from Route 23 and then Route 395, the **Unaka Mountain Auto Tour❖** loops for 30 miles through a section of Cherokee National Forest. Here again are the puzzling balds. Beauty Spot Gap is at an elevation of 4,500 feet along the eastern segment of the tour adjacent to the North Carolina border. Nearby is the 4,700-acre **Unaka Mountain Wilderness❖,** where vehicles are prohibited but trails lead to virgin eastern hemlocks, the 60-foot Red Fork Falls, and numerous other waterfalls. Farther along an overlook provides a view of North Carolina's **Mount Mitchell,** which at 6,684 feet is the highest point east of the Mississippi. The spruce-fir forest in these uplands harbors the endangered Carolina northern flying squirrel and the Appalachian salamander, which lays its eggs on the forest floor instead of in a stream or river. Little light filters through the dense woods, and the lungless salamander finds an unusual haven of high moisture.

Some 20 miles southwest of Erwin, off Route 208, the gravel-and-dirt Forest Service Road 41 leads into the forest and, about 2 miles in, passes a totally exposed, textbook example of a small asymmetrical fold in the rock. Some 16 major layers follow the graceful lines of the deep fold, which resembles a V exaggerated so that the point is squeezed beyond the vertical to slant leftward. Across the road, Paint Creek tracks through a thick conifer and hardwood forest punctuated by innumerable rhododendron thickets.

THE BOUNTIFUL SMOKIES

Superlatives abound at **Great Smoky Mountains National Park❖**. Elevations range from 840 feet to 6,643 feet (at Clingmans Dome), and 27 peaks and other features rise higher than 6,000 feet. A botanical showcase, the park protects more than 1,500 kinds of flowering plants, including about 100 species of native trees. Some 200 species of birds live here—and more than 70 of them are winter inhabitants. Among the 70 mammal species are black bears and 24 native rodents; about 60 kinds of fish dwell in the streams. There are 23 types of snakes (only the timber rattlesnake and copperhead are poisonous), a dozen species of toads and frogs, and 27 kinds of salamanders—the greatest number of any place in North America—and one of them, the red-cheeked salamander, lives only within the park. With all these attributes, it is no wonder that the park is both an international biosphere reserve and a world heritage site.

This variety exists because the Appalachians run on a northeast-southwest axis. When northern species moved south ahead of the Ice Age glaciers, they found a haven in the Great Smokies, while many warm-climate species moved north because they were not blocked by an east-west–running barrier. As the climate warmed, the northern species remained by moving to cooler habitats higher up the mountains while the southern species retreated to the warmer lower elevations.

Another reason for the bountiful flora and fauna is rain: The Smokies receive more than 80 inches of precipitation on the peaks and 50 inches in the valleys each year, making the region one of the wettest in the contiguous United States. More than half of the precipitation is absorbed in the ground to become part of the countless natural springs or the 300 streams and rivers that flow all year. The rest of the rain evaporates or is used directly by plants and trees, which in turn provide food for the diverse wildlife.

ABOVE: *Depending on its location in the southern mountains, the Appalachian woodland salamander's markings differ. In the Great Smokies, it is known as the red-cheeked salamander for obvious reasons.*

Those who cannot travel the entire Appalachian Trail from Georgia to Maine may hike, with judicious detours, from Cades Cove to Clingmans Dome in the park and see roughly the same variety of forests. The same can be done by driving from park headquarters near Gatlinburg to Newfound Gap on the Tennessee–North Carolina border. Each gain of 100 feet in elevation represents roughly 17 miles of northward progress. A traveler can ascend from oak-pine forests characteristic of northern Georgia, to oak-hickory-red maple typical of Virginia through Massachusetts, to the spruce-fir woods of Maine. Keep that in mind when planning a visit, for spring in the Smokies comes six weeks earlier in the lower elevations than in the higher ones.

With all these glorious natural riches, it is difficult to believe that about 75 percent of the Smokies' forests were logged over in the late 1800s and early 1900s. However, the remaining 25 percent of the park's 520,000 acres still represented the most extensive virgin forests

OVERLEAF: *Most lands within Great Smoky Mountains National Park have reverted to woodland, but the fields in Cades Cove are still hayed or grazed to provide a reminder of former farming communities.*

in the eastern United States when the park was established in the 1930s. Since then second-growth forests have claimed most of the overlogged or overgrazed lands that Tennessee and North Carolina purchased from about 6,000 owners. It is the trees that give off water vapor and hydrocarbons that contribute to the distinctive blue haze that often floats above the landscape. The Cherokee called their homeland "Shaconage," the place of blue smoke, in tribute to this veil that hangs over the forests, meadows, and mountains.

So where and when should a visitor go to see all these natural treasures? The park is the most heavily visited U.S. national park, and the crowds are especially thick during the spring blooming season, the summer school-vacation season, and the colorful foliage season, which peaks in early October at the higher elevations and mid-October at the lower elevations.

The Great Smoky Mountains Natural History Association sells brochures listing favorite trails, advising about where to see specific kinds of forests and particular flowering plants and shrubs, and pinpointing waterfalls and other natural features. A visitor can find a cove hardwood forest on a trail at the Chimney Tops Picnic Area, hike to Silers Bald or Andrews Bald or through a spruce-fir forest in the Clingmans Dome area, or climb to 60-foot Indian Creek Falls from Deep Creek Road. Dogwood and redbud bloom from mid- to late April, spring flowers from late March to mid-May, flame azalea and mountain laurel in May and June, and catawba rhododendron in mid-June. Park interpreters hold many evening programs and nature walks. The park, with its more than 800 miles of maintained trails, including 70 miles of the Appalachian Trail, is a backpacker's dream, and there are many short trails with delightful features for casual day-trippers. Rangers can advise about trails and conditions.

However, all is not well in the park. Ten million human visitors, most in automobiles, come each year, and area tourist facilities continually expand to meet the demand. The total effects of crowding and overuse are yet to be fully determined. At the same time, the wild hog is causing heavy damage rooting up the earth and plants and sullying streams, the rainbow and brown trout are overtaking the habitat of the native brook trout, a fungus is killing hundreds of thousands of dogwoods, and an exotic insect, the balsam woolly adelgid, has de-

In 1940, 10,000 people joined President Franklin Roosevelt to open Great Smoky Mountains National Park (top right). For the park, engineers opened up the mountainous terrain with a loop-over bridge that replaced four sharp curves (top left) and introduced paved roads into the isolated valley of Cades Cove (bottom).

stroyed 95 percent of the mature Fraser firs. Park managers, ever conscious of the blight that killed off the once-prevalent chestnut trees, have their hands full. They can, however, cite some positive signs. The black bear population in the park has rebounded and now numbers 400 to 500. White-tailed deer are again numerous, and river otters and red wolves are being gradually reintroduced. Reports of panther sightings, though not conclusive, are persistent.

A nice last stop in the park, the meadows and old homesteads of Cades Cove provide a respite from the rigors of steep mountains, arduous trails, and thick forests. Deer come to graze in such numbers that on any given morning there may be 40 of them in various groupings within a half mile. From Cades Cove, the rugged, one-way Rich Mountain Road provides a convenient exit—except in the winter—

from the northwest corner of the national park back into the Cherokee National Forest's southern section.

CHEROKEE NATIONAL FOREST—SOUTH

It is wise to have U.S. Forest Service maps when traveling in the **Cherokee National Forest❖,** especially its southern section, as the state's official highway map is not detailed for this corner of the state. From Route 411 south of Maryville, Route 360 leads to Tellico Plains. With the great mountains now presiding at a distance, the topography is less dramatic. The U.S. Forest Service's Tellico District forests are about 60 percent hardwoods, with pines sweeping across the drier ridgetops and southern slopes.

From Tellico Plains, drive ten miles eastward into the forest on Route 165 and Forest Road 210 for seven miles to the 3,721-acre **Bald River Gorge Wilderness❖.** Although the 120-foot Bald River Falls can be seen from along the road, a pleasant trail from Holly Flats Recreation Area flanks the river, reaching the falls and passing many scenic cascades. A remote gravel road marked 384 provides a rugged 11-mile route through Bald River Gorge and its hilltop forests, dotted with fleabane and black-eyed Susans, to Route 68 near **Coker Creek Scenic Area❖.** A brief gold rush ensued after nuggets were found in this Unicoi Mountains creek in 1831, but it is estimated that less than $250,000 worth of gold was panned from the creek over the years. The scenic area is only 375 acres, but old-growth hemlocks, flame azaleas, mountain laurels, and waterfalls are fine rewards for strenuous hiking.

Bordering North Carolina is **Citico Creek Wilderness❖,** at 15,891 acres the largest designated wilderness in the national forest and an enclave for the black bear. Four trails that total more than 20 miles wind through this roadless wild terrain, which includes numerous waterfalls, most notably the 80-foot Falls Branch Falls.

Route 315 winds through the 2,493-acre **Gee Creek Wilderness❖,** with three primitive hiking trails, to the towns of Springtown and Reliance, where **Hiwassee Scenic River** flows peacefully beside Route

---

RIGHT: *The Middle Prong of the Little River rushes over boulders amid black gum and maple trees decked out in autumn's brilliant hues. Colors peak in the Smokies between mid-September and mid-October.*

30. A 23-mile stretch of the Hiwassee has been designated a scenic river by the state. From the North Carolina border to Route 411 north of Benton the river is rated class III for rafting, but much of the remainder is rated an easy class I or II. Originating in the Blue Ridge Mountains in north Georgia near the Appalachian Trail, the river provides drainage for 750,000 acres, and because 90 percent of the Hiwassee runs through heavily forested areas, the waters are particularly clean. The southern section of the **John Muir Trail** follows the Hiwassee for 17 miles from a trailhead off Forest Road 108 near Reliance. Although currently incomplete, the trail honors the naturalist's 1,000-mile walk through Tennessee in 1867. Canoe accesses to the river are nearby. Some three dozen bird species here include the semipalmated plover and several terns.

South of the Hiwassee, Route 64/74 runs between Cleveland and Ducktown and with Forest Road 77 makes up the 26-mile **Ocoee Scenic Byway** along the Ocoee River, one of the major kayaking, canoeing, and rafting rivers in the United States and site of the 1996 Olympic white-water competitions. The river owes its popularity to its boulder-strewn rapids and to fairly regular TVA-controlled releases of water. Forest Road 77 is a spur road that leads up to the 2,200-foot level of Chilhowee Mountain, ending just 400 feet short of the summit. It is a particularly spectacular—and popular—destination in fall foliage season.

Ducktown and Copperhill, in the southeastern tip of Tennessee, were denuded of trees after copper ore was discovered along Potato Creek in 1843. A huge extracting and smelting industry operated here until 1987, leaving a 50-square-mile scar of reddish soil. Much of the land was then reforested, a program that ended when some local residents protested that they liked the red hills and felt that a slice of the state's history should be preserved even if some found industry's scar unattractive. The Ducktown Basin Museum tells the full story. That highly unnatural area, with its inherent environmental preservation message, closes this tour of Tennessee's natural regions.

LEFT: *A fine view of Ramsay Cascades, the highest waterfall in Great Smoky Mountains National Park, rewards hikers in the Greenbrier area.*
OVERLEAF: *From Newfound Gap, the Great Smokies sweep to the horizon in a wondrous panorama of mountains and valleys, trees and sky.*

FURTHER READING ABOUT CENTRAL APPALACHIA

Audubon Field Guides. New York: Knopf, 1970s through 1990s. This series of illustrated guides encompasses more than 17 titles covering North American birds, mammals, wildflowers, insects and spiders, reptiles and amphibians, trees, and more.

BERRY, WENDELL. *The Unforeseen Wilderness: Kentucky's Red River Gorge.* San Francisco: North Point Press, 1991. Essayist pays both a philosophical and down-to-earth tribute to an area threatened by a dam.

BROOKS, MAURICE. *The Appalachians.* Boston: Houghton Mifflin, 1965. This easygoing (but out-of-print) masterpiece about the natural history of the Appalachians is well worth a trip to the library or used-book store.

CAUDILL, HARRY M. *Night Comes to the Cumberlands: A Biography of a Depressed Area.* Boston: Little, Brown, 1962. A classic about the devastating effects of coal mining on Kentucky and its people.

CONSTANTZ, GEORGE. *Hollows, Peepers, and Highlanders: An Appalachian Ecology.* Missoula, MT: Mountain Press Publishing Co., 1994. In short, delightful essays, an "unabashed partisan of the Appalachian Mountains" from West Virginia examines balds, salamanders, brook trout, and other wildlife.

DYKEMAN, WILMA. *Tennessee: A Bicentennial History.* New York: Norton, 1975. A marvelous storyteller romps through the history of three states in one— East, Middle, and West Tennessee.

DYKEMAN, WILMA, AND JIM STOKELY. *At Home in the Smokies: A History Handbook for Great Smoky Mountains National Park.* Washington, D.C.: National Park Service, 1984. Although focused on the people who settled along Tennessee's border with North Carolina, this book conveys a sense of what it was like to live in the middle and southern Appalachians in the late 1800s and early 1900s.

HOUK, ROSE. *Great Smoky Mountains National Park: A Natural History Guide.* New York: Houghton Mifflin Co., 1993. This highly accessible guidebook is full of practical information, plus insights into current wildlife management issues and programs.

HUDSON, PATRICIA L., AND SANDRA L. BALLARD. *The Smithsonian Guide to Historic America: The Carolinas and the Appalachian States.* New York: Stewart, Tabori & Chang, 1989. A companion to the natural areas volume, this guide describes the historic sites in West Virginia, Kentucky, and Tennessee, plus the Carolinas.

MANNING, RUSS. *The Historic Cumberland Plateau: An Explorer's Guide.* Knoxville: University of Tennessee Press, 1993. The author, a naturalist, delves into the plateau's geology and zoology and provides sound on-the-ground advice for hikers and motorists.

MCCAGUE, JAMES. *The Cumberland.* New York: Holt, Rinehart and Winston, 1973. Spiced with folktales, this volume in the Rivers of America series gives a good feel for the roles that Native Americans, Daniel Boone, Andrew Jackson, and others played in our national heritage.

McPHEE, JOHN. *In Suspect Terrain.* New York: Farrar, Straus & Giroux, 1983. For an understanding of plate tectonics and the Appalachians, travel along with this writer for the *New Yorker* magazine.

PORTER, ELIOT, AND EDWARD ABBEY. *Appalachian Wilderness: The Great Smoky Mountains.* New York: Ballantine Books, 1973. A coffee-table book of subtle Porter photographs juxtaposed with a mildly irreverent Abbey text.

STUART, JESSE. *The Best-Loved Short Stories of Jesse Stuart.* New York: McGraw-Hill, 1982. A collection of stories by a teacher-author-poet who wrote about his neighbors and the Kentucky farm where he grew up.

WILLIAMS, JOHN ALEXANDER. *West Virginia: A Bicentennial History.* New York: Norton, 1984. From little-known disasters and incidents to major events and legendary feuds, a historian looks at the Mountain State's varied past.

WILSON, JENNIFER BAUER. *Roan Mountain: A Passage of Time.* Winston-Salem: John F. Blair Publisher, 1991. A ranger-naturalist eloquently tells the natural and human history of a mountain.

WUERTHNER, GEORGE. *Southern Appalachian Country.* Helena, MT: American Geographic Publishing, 1990. A photographer-naturalist travels through the mountains examining the diverse wildlife in different habitats.

ABOVE: *Civil War troops mass in Harpers Ferry, site of the famed John Brown raid and confluence of the Potomac and Shenandoah rivers.*

GLOSSARY

alluvial plain deposit of alluvium: gravel, sand, and smaller materials that have formed a plain, usually at the base of mountains; created by water rushing down a mountain

biotic pertaining to plants and animals

bluff cliff, or steep wall of rock or soil, that borders a river or floodplain; created as the water erodes the riverbank

coniferous describing the cone-bearing trees of the pine family; usually evergreen

deciduous describing trees that shed leaves seasonally and remain leafless for part of the year

delta flat, low-lying plain that forms at the mouth of a river as the river slows and deposits sediment gathered upstream

edaphic ecological condition related to or caused by the soil conditions of a particular area

endemic having originated in and being restricted to one particular environment

escarpment cliff or steep rock face, formed by faulting or fracturing of the earth's crust, that separates two comparatively level land surfaces

fault break in the earth's outermost layer, or crust, along which rock may move against rock

igneous referring to rock formed by cooled and hardened lava

isthmus narrow strip of land connecting two larger land areas and separating two bodies of water

karst topography land lying over limestone that is dotted with sinkholes, underground streams, and caves formed as rainwater erodes the soft rock

metamorphic referring to a rock that has been changed into its present state after being subjected to heat, pressure, or chemical change

oxbow lake lake that forms where a meandering river overflows and forms a crescent-shaped body of standing water; called an oxbow because its curved shape looks like the U-shaped harness frame that fits around an ox's neck

plates thick slabs of rock that make up the earth's outer shell, including the ocean floor and the continental landmasses; movement and interaction of the plates is known as plate tectonics

rain shadow area of dry land on the side of a mountain facing away from the moisture-laden winds blowing inland from the ocean

rapids broken, fast-flowing water that tumbles around boulders; classified from I to VI according to increasing difficulty of watercraft navigation

ravine narrow, steep-sided valley that has been eroded by running water

sedimentary rocks formed from deposits of small eroded debris such as gravel, sand, mud, silt, or peat

sinkhole funnel-shaped hole where water has collected in the cracks of limestone, dissolved the rock, and carried it away; also formed when roofs of caves collapse

sphagnum moss that grows in wet, acidic areas; decomposes and compacts to form peat

wetland area of land covered or saturated with groundwater; includes swamps, marshes, and bogs

LAND MANAGEMENT RESOURCES

The following public and private organizations are among the important administrators of the preserved and protected areas described in this volume. Brief explanations of the various legal and legislative designations of these areas follow.

MANAGING ORGANIZATIONS

Kentucky Department of Fish and Wildlife Resources
Responsible for the management and protection of fish and wildlife within 72 wildlife management areas. Issues state hunting and fishing licenses.

Kentucky Department of Parks
Manages 49 recreational parks, resort parks, and historic sites. Part of the Kentucky Tourism Cabinet.

Kentucky Division of Forestry
Manages 30,000 acres of state forest for recreation, wildlife, timber, and water. Also works with private landowners to maintain a balanced stewardship of forest lands. Division of Kentucky Natural Resources and Environmental Protection Cabinet.

Kentucky State Nature Preserves Commission
Owns and manages 31 nature preserves, totalling 10,272 acres, for conservation and recreation. Division of Kentucky Natural Resources and Environmental Protection Cabinet.

National Park Service (NPS) Department of the Interior
Regulates the use of national parks, monuments, and preserves. Resources are managed to preserve and protect landscape, natural and historic artifacts, and wildlife. Also administers historic and national landmarks, national seashores, wild and scenic rivers, and the national trail system.

The Nature Conservancy (TNC) Private Organization
International nonprofit organization that owns the largest private system of nature sanctuaries in the world, some 1,300 preserves. Aims to preserve significant plant, animal, and natural communities. Some areas are managed by other private or public conservation groups, other areas by the Conservancy itself.

Tennessee Division of Forestry
Manages more than 150,000 acres of land in 13 state forests for multiple uses, including recreation and timber production. Division of the Department of Agriculture.

Tennessee State Parks
Manages 50 state parks, including natural areas, historic sites, and resort and recreational parks. Part of the Department of Environment and Conservation.

Tennessee Wildlife Resources Agency
Manages 78 wildlife management areas and numerous wetlands and refuges for conservation, hunting, and fishing. Issues hunting and fishing licenses and boating registrations.

U.S. Fish and Wildlife Service (USFWS) Department of the Interior

Principal federal agency responsible for conserving, protecting, and enhancing the country's fish and wildlife and their habitats. Manages national wildlife refuges, fish hatcheries, and programs for migratory birds and endangered species.

U.S. Forest Service (USFS) Department of Agriculture

Administers more than 190 million acres in the national forests and national grasslands and is responsible for the management of their resources. Determines how best to combine commercial uses such as grazing, mining, and logging with conservation needs.

West Virginia Division of Natural Resources

Administers all state parks, forests, and wildlife management areas. Also issues hunting and fishing licenses and boating regulations.

DESIGNATIONS

Archaeological Area

Area of significant archaeological interest and resources that may contribute to the study of prehistory. Managed by the federal Bureau of Land Management (BLM) or individual states.

Geological Area

Land so designated because of its geological significance. Area of importance is generally readily accessible for viewing. Managed by the USFS.

National Forest

Large acreage managed for the use of forests, watersheds, wildlife, and recreation by the public and private sectors. Managed by the USFS.

National Historical Park

Land designated to preserve an area of national historic significance. Managed by the NPS.

National Military Park

Park set aside to commemorate its association with some aspect of American military history. Managed by the NPS.

National Park

Spacious primitive or wilderness area with scenery and natural wonders so outstanding it has been preserved by the federal government, primarily for recreational use. Managed by the NPS.

National Recreation Area

Site established to conserve and develop for recreational purposes an area of scenic, natural, or historic interest. Powerboats, dirt and mountain bikes, and ORVs allowed with restrictions. Managed by the NPS.

National Recreation Trail

Created by the National Trails System Act of 1968 to provide outdoor recreation trails for public use, in or near urban areas. Managed by the NPS.

National Scenic Trail

Created by the National Trails System Act of 1968 to provide long-distance public recreational trails through nationally significant scenic, historic, natural, or cultural areas. Managed by the NPS.

National Wildlife Refuge

Public land set aside for wild animals; protects migratory waterfowl, endangered and threatened species, and native plants and their habitat. Managed by USFWS.

Natural Area

Area designated and preserved in its natural state for its exceptional value in displaying the natural history of the United States. Managed by individual states.

Nature Preserve

Area that protects specific natural resources. Hunting, fishing, and mining may be permitted. Managed by the NPS and local or state authorities.

Wild and Scenic River

National program set up to preserve selected rivers, chosen for their outstanding scenic, recreational, geologic, wildlife, historic, or archaeological features, in their natural free-flowing condition, as well as to develop other rivers for hydropower purposes. Management shared by BLM, NPS, and USFWS.

Wilderness Area

Area with particular ecological, geological, scientific, scenic, or historical value that has been set aside in its natural condition to be preserved as wild land; limited recreational use is permitted. Managed by the BLM and NPS.

Wildlife Management Area

Land managed or owned by the state to protect wildlife. Aside from seasonal restrictions, hunting, fishing, and public access are allowed. Managed by individual states.

NATURE TRAVEL

The following is a selection of national and local organizations that sponsor nature-related travel activities or can provide specialized regional travel information.

NATIONAL

National Audubon Society
700 Broadway
New York, NY 10003
(212) 979-3000
Offers a wide range of ecological field studies, tours, and cruises throughout the United States

National Wildlife Federation
1400 16th St. NW
Washington D.C. 20036
(703) 790-4363
Offers training in environmental education for all ages, wildlife camp and teen adventures, and conservation summits involving nature walks, field trips, and classes

The Nature Conservancy
1815 North Lynn St.
Arlington, VA 22209
(703) 841-5300
Offers a variety of excursions based out of regional and state offices. May include hiking, backpacking, canoeing, horseback riding. Contact above number to locate state offices

Sierra Club Outings
730 Polk St.
San Francisco, CA 94109
(415) 923-5630
Offers tours of different lengths for all ages throughout the United States. Outings may include backpacking, hiking, biking, skiing, and water excursions

Smithsonian Study Tours and Seminars
1100 Jefferson Dr. SW
MRC 702
Washington, D.C. 20560
(202) 357-4700
Offers extended tours, cruises, research expeditions, and seminars throughout the United States

REGIONAL

Appalachian Trail Conference
PO Box 807
Harpers Ferry, WV 25425
(304) 535-6331
Coordinates the preservation and management of the 2,100-mile Appalachian Trail, including trails through Tennessee and West Virginia. Prepares and distributes guidebooks and related trail and hiking information

Kentucky Department of Travel Development
500 Mero St., Ste. 2200
Frankfort, KY 40601
(800) 225-8747 (TRIP)
Publishes and distributes travel information. Answers specific travel, recreation, and accommodation questions.

Oglebay Institute
A. B. Brooks Nature Center
Oglebay Park
Wheeling, WV 26003
(304) 242-6855
Nonprofit nature center that organizes and leads nature walks and weekend nature seminars focusing on West Virginia's natural history

Tennessee Department of Tourism
PO Box 23170
Nashville, TN 37202
(615) 741-2159
(800) 836-6200 (for brochure)
Distributes vacation guides and maps. Answers specific travel-related queries

West Virginia Tourism
1900 Kanawha Blvd. E.
Bldg. 6, Room B-564
Charleston, WV 25305
(800) CALL WVA (225-5982)
Offers travel and vacation brochures. Operators can answer specific travel questions

HOW TO USE THIS SITE GUIDE

The following site information guide will assist you in planning your tour of the natural areas of West Virginia, Tennessee, and Kentucky. Sites set in boldface and followed by the symbol ❖ in the text are here organized alphabetically by state. Each entry is followed by the mailing address (sometimes different from the street address) and phone number of the immediate managing office, plus brief notes and a list of facilities and activities available. (A key appears on each page.)

Information on hours of operation, seasonal closings, and fees is often not listed, as these vary from season to season and year to year. Please bear in mind that responsibility for the management of some sites may change. Call well in advance to obtain maps, brochures, and pertinent, up-to-date information that will help you plan your adventures in Central Appalachia.

Each site entry in the guide includes the address and phone number of its immediate managing agency. Many of these sites are under the stewardship of a forest or park ranger or supervised from a small nearby office. Hence, in many cases, those sites will be difficult to contact directly, and it is preferable to call the managing agency.

The following umbrella organizations can provide general information for individual natural sites, as well as the area as a whole:

KENTUCKY

Dept. of Fish and Wildlife Resources
1 Game Farm Road
Frankfort, KY 40601
(502) 564-3400

Dept. of Parks
Capitol Plaza Tower
10th Floor
Frankfort, KY 40601
(502) 564-2172

National Park Service
75 Spring St. SW
Atlanta, GA 30303
(404) 331-5185

U.S. Forest Service
1720 Peachtree Rd. NW
Atlanta, GA 30367
(404) 347-4177

TENNESSEE

Dept. of Environment and Conservation
401 Church St.
Nashville, TN 37243
(615) 532-0109

National Park Service
75 Spring St. SW
Atlanta, GA 30303
(404) 331-5185

U.S. Forest Service
1720 Peachtree Rd. NW
Atlanta, GA 30367
(404) 347-4177

Wildlife Resources Agency
PO Box 40747
Ellington Agricultural Center
Nashville, TN 37204
(615) 781-6500

WEST VIRGINIA

Division of Natural Resources
1900 Kanawha Blvd. E
Charleston, WV 25305
(304) 558-2754

National Park Service
200 Chestnut St.
Philadelphia, PA 19106
(215) 597-7013

U.S. Fish and Wildlife Service
300 Westgate Center Dr.
Hadley, MA 01035
(413) 253-8200

U.S. Forest Service
310 W. Wisconsin Ave.
Milwaukee, WI 53203
(414) 297-3600

KENTUCKY

BAD BRANCH STATE NATURE PRESERVE
Kentucky State
Nature Preserves Commission
801 Schenkel Lane
Frankfort, KY 40601
(502) 573-2886   **BW, H, MT**

**BALLARD COUNTY WILDLIFE
MANAGEMENT AREA**
Kentucky Dept. of Fish
and Wildlife Resources
Rte. 1, Box 84
La Center, KY 42056
(502) 224-2244   **BW, C, F, H, HR, I, PA**

**BEAVER CREEK WILDLIFE
MANAGEMENT AREA**
Kentucky Dept. of Fish
and Wildlife Resources
HC 84, Box 820
Parkers Lake, KY 42634
(606) 376-8083   **BW, C, F, H, MT, S**

**BERNHEIM ARBORETUM AND
RESEARCH FOREST**
Isaac W. Bernheim Foundation
Rte. 245, Clermont, KY 40110
(502) 955-8512
    Day use only; open 7 days; admission
    fee on weekends; guides on weekends
            BW, F, H, I, MT, PA, RA, T, TG

BIG BONE LICK STATE PARK
Kentucky Dept. of Parks
3380 Beaver Rd.
Union, KY 41091
(606) 384-3522
(606) 384-3906   **C, F, GS, H, PA**

**BIG SOUTH FORK NATIONAL RIVER AND
RECREATION AREA**
National Park Service
Rte. 3, Box 401
Oneida, TN 37841
(615) 879-3625
        **BT, BW, C, CK, F, GS, H, HR, I, L,
        MB, MT, PA, RA, RC, S, T, TG**

BLUE LICKS BATTLEFIELD STATE PARK
Kentucky Dept. of Parks
PO Box 66
Mount Olivet, KY 41064
(606) 289-5507
            C, F, GS, H, L, MT, PA, S, T

**BOONE COUNTY CLIFFS STATE
NATURE PRESERVE**
Kentucky State
Nature Preserves Commission
801 Schenkel Lane
Frankfort, KY 40601
(502) 573-2886   **BW, H, MT**

BREAKS INTERSTATE PARK
Breaks Interstate Park Commission
PO Box 100
Breaks, VA 24607
(703) 865-4413; (800) 982-5122
            **BT, BW, C, CK, F, GS, H, HR,
            I, L, MT, PA, RA, S, T, TG**

**CANE CREEK WILDLIFE
MANAGEMENT AREA**
Kentucky Dept. of Fish
and Wildlife Resources
1 Game Farm Rd.
Frankfort, KY 40601
(502) 564-4406 (wildlife office)
(606) 745-3100 (forest office)
    Some primitive camping allowed; check
    with forest office first
                        BW, C, F, H, MT

CARTER CAVES STATE RESORT PARK
Kentucky Dept. of Parks
Rte. 5, Olive Hill, KY 41164
Fee for cave tours   **BW, C, CK, F, GS,
            H, HR, I, L, MT, PA, RA, S, T, TG**

CLAY WILDLIFE MANAGEMENT AREA
Kentucky Dept. of Fish
and Wildlife Resources
1449 Cassidy Creek Rd.
Carlisle, KY 40311
(606) 289-2564
    Nature walk; no ORVs; primitive camping
                            BW, C, F, H, HR

CLIFTY WILDERNESS
Daniel Boone National Forest
Stanton Ranger District
705 West College Ave.
Stanton, KY 40380
(606) 663-2852
            BW, C, F, H, HR, MT, RC, XC

CLYDE E. BUCKLEY WILDLIFE SANCTUARY
National Audubon Society
1305 Germany Rd.
Frankfort, KY 40601
(606) 873-5711

BT Bike Trails	**CK** Canoeing,	**F** Fishing	**HR** Horseback
BW Bird-watching	Kayaking	**GS** Gift Shop	Riding
C Camping	**DS** Downhill	**H** Hiking	**I** Information
	Skiing		Center

264

Includes nature center; hours of operation vary; check with office

BW, GS, H, I, MT, PA, RA, T, TG

COLUMBUS-BELMONT STATE PARK
Kentucky Dept. of Parks
PO Box 8, Columbus, KY 42032
(502) 677-2327

BW, C, GS, H, I, MT, PA, T

CRANKS CREEK
WILDLIFE MANAGEMENT AREA
Kentucky Dept. of Fish
and Wildlife Resources
1 Game Farm Rd.
Frankfort, KY 40601
(502) 564-4406   **BW, F, H, MT, PA**

CUMBERLAND FALLS STATE RESORT PARK
Kentucky Dept. of Parks
7351 Rte. 90
Corbin, KY 40701
(606) 528-4121   **BW, C, CK, F, GS, H,
                          HR, I, L, MT, PA, S, T, TG**

CUMBERLAND GAP
NATIONAL HISTORICAL PARK
National Park Service
PO Box 1848, Middlesboro, KY 40965
(606) 248-2817
   Includes Pinnacle Overlook; visitor center near Middlesboro

**BT, BW, C, GS, I,
MT, RA, T, TG**

CUMBERLAND TRAIL
c/o Cumberland Gap
National Historical Park
PO Box 1848
Middlesboro, KY 40965
(606) 248-2817   **BW, H, MT**

DALE HOLLOW
LAKE STATE PARK
Kentucky Dept. of Parks
6371 State Park Rd.
Bow, KY 42714
(502) 433-7431   **BT, BW, C, F, H, HR,
                          I, MB, MT, PA, S, T**

DALE HOLLOW
WILDLIFE MANAGEMENT AREA
Kentucky Dept. of
Fish and Wildlife Resources
1 Game Farm Rd.
Frankfort, KY 40601
(502) 564-4406   **BW, C, F, MT, T**

DANIEL BOONE NATIONAL FOREST
U.S. Forest Service
1700 Bypass Rd.
Winchester, KY 40391
(606) 745-3100
**BT, BW, C, CK, F, H, HR, I,
MB, MT, PA, RC, S, T, XC**

GREENBO LAKE STATE RESORT PARK
Kentucky Dept. of Parks
HC 60, Box 562
Greenup, KY 41144
(606) 473-7324   **BW, C, CK, F, GS, H, L,
                    MT, PA, RA, S, T**

GREEN RIVER LAKE STATE PARK
Kentucky Dept. of Parks
179 Park Office Rd.
Campbellsville, KY 42718
(502) 465-8255
BT, C, F, GS, H, MT, PA, S, T

GREEN RIVER
WILDLIFE MANAGEMENT AREA
Kentucky Dept. of Fish
and Wildlife Resources
3750 Palestine Rd.
Campbellsville, KY 42718
(502) 465-4039   **BW, CK, F, H**

JENNY WILEY
NATIONAL RECREATION TRAIL
Kentucky Dept. of Parks
Div. of Recreation and Interpretation
Capital Plaza Tower
Frankfort, KY 40601
(502) 564-2172
   Facilities at 3 state parks; bikes allowed
   on paved parts of trail only; primitive
   camping at designated areas only
BW, C, F, H, I, L, MB, MT, PA, S, T, TG

JENNY WILEY STATE RESORT PARK
Kentucky Dept. of Parks
39 Jenny Wiley Rd.
Prestonburg, KY 41653
(606) 886-2711; (800) 325-0142
**BW, C, F, GS, H, L, MT,
PA, RA, S, T, TG**

JESSE STUART STATE NATURE PRESERVE
Kentucky State Nature Preserves
Commission
801 Schenkel Lane
Frankfort, KY 40601
(502) 573-2886   **BW, H, MT**

L	Lodging	**PA** Picnic Areas	**RC** Rock Climbing	**TG** Tours, Guides
MB	Mountain Biking	**RA** Ranger-led Activities	**S** Swimming	**XC** Cross-country Skiing
MT	Marked Trails		**T** Toilets	

JOHN A. KLEBER
WILDLIFE MANAGEMENT AREA
Kentucky Dept. of Fish
and Wildlife Resources
5010 Cedar Rd.
Owenton, KY 40359
(502) 535-6335
BT, BW, C, F, H, HR, I, MB, PA, XC

JOHN JAMES AUDUBON STATE PARK
Kentucky Dept. of Parks
PO Box 576, Henderson, KY 42420
(800) 255-7275; (502) 827-1893
(502) 573-2886 (preserve)
Includes state nature preserve
BW, C, F, GS, H, L, MT, PA, S, T, TG

KALER BOTTOMS
WILDLIFE MANAGEMENT AREA
Kentucky Dept. of Fish
and Wildlife Resources
1 Game Farm Rd.
Frankfort, KY 40601
(502) 564-4406
Swampy area   **BW, CK, F, H, HR**

KENLAKE STATE
RESORT PARK
Kentucky Dept. of Parks
542 Kenlake Rd.
Hardin, KY 42048
(800) 325-0143
BW, C, F, GS, H, L, PA, S

KENTENIA STATE FOREST
Kentucky Div. of Forestry
627 Comanche Trail
Frankfort, KY 40601
(502) 564-4496
BW, C, F, H, HR, MB, PA, T, XC

KENTUCKY DAM VILLAGE
STATE RESORT PARK
Kentucky Dept. of Parks
PO Box 69, Gilbertsville, KY 44204
(502) 362-4271
C, F, GS, HR, L, PA, S

KENTUCKY RIDGE
STATE FOREST
Kentucky Div. of Forestry
627 Comanche Trail
Frankfort, KY 40601
(502) 564-4496
BW, C, F, H, HR, MB, XC

KINGDOM COME STATE PARK
Kentucky Dept. of Parks
PO Box M
Cumberland, KY 40823
(606) 589-2479
Includes Little Shepherd Trail
BW, C, F, GS, H, HR, MB, MT, PA, T, TG

LAKE BARKLEY STATE RESORT PARK
Kentucky Dept. of Parks
PO Box 790
Cadiz, KY 42211
(800) 325-1708; (502) 924-1131
BW, C, CK, F, GS, H, HR, L, MT, PA, S, T

LAKE CUMBERLAND STATE RESORT PARK
Kentucky Dept. of Parks
5465 State Park Rd.
Jamestown, KY 42629
(502) 343-3111
BT, BW, C, F, GS, H, HR, I, L, MT, PA, RA, S, T

LAKE CUMBERLAND WILDLIFE
MANAGEMENT AREA
U.S. Army Corps of Engineers
HC 84, Box 820
Parker's Lake, KY 42634
(606) 376-8083   **BW, F, H, S**

LAND BETWEEN THE LAKES
Tennessee Valley Authority
100 Van Morgan Dr.
Golden Pond, KY 42211-9001
(502) 924-5602
BT, BW, C, CK, F, GS, H, HR, I, MB, MT, PA, RA, S, T, TG

LEVI JACKSON STATE PARK
Kentucky Dept. of Parks
998 Levi Jackson Mill Mill Rd.
London, KY 40741
(606) 878-8000
BW, C, GS, H, MT, PA, S

LILLEY CORNETT WOODS
Eastern Kentucky University
HC 63, Box 2710, Skyline, KY 41821
(606) 633-5828   **BW, H, I, PA, T, TG**

LITTLE SHEPHERD TRAIL
c/o Kingdom Come State Park
PO Box M
Cumberland, KY 40823
(606) 589-2479   **BT, BW, F, H, MB**

BT Bike Trails	**CK** Canoeing, Kayaking	**F** Fishing	**HR** Horseback Riding
BW Bird-watching	**DS** Downhill Skiing	**GS** Gift Shop	**I** Information Center
C Camping		**H** Hiking	

MAMMOTH CAVE NATIONAL PARK
National Park Service
Mammoth Cave, KY 42259
(502) 758-2328
(800) 967-2283 (reservations)
Recommend reservations for cave tour
**BT, BW, C, CK, F, GS, H, HR,
I, L, MT, PA, RA, T, TG**

METROPOLIS LAKE
STATE NATURE PRESERVE
Kentucky State
Nature Preserves Commission
801 Schenkel Lane, Frankfort, KY 40601
(502) 573-2886 **BW, H, MT**

MILL CREEK
WILDLIFE MANAGEMENT AREA
Kentucky Dept. of Fish
and Wildlife Resources
1 Game Farm Rd., Frankfort, KY 40601
(606) 986-8434
Primitive camping
**BT, BW, C, CK, F, H, HR,
MB, MT, PA, RC, T**

NATURAL BRIDGE STATE RESORT PARK
Kentucky Dept. of Parks
2135 Natural Bridge Rd.
Slade, KY 40376
(606) 663-2214; (800) 325-1710
Trails are steep and rocky
**BW, C, F, GS, H, I, L,
MT, PA, RA, S, T, TG**

NOLIN LAKE PUBLIC WILDLIFE AREA
Kentucky Dept. of Fish
and Wildlife Resources
1 Game Farm Rd., Frankfort, KY 40601-3908
(502) 286-4511
BW, C, CK, F, H, HR, I, PA, S, T

PEAL WILDLIFE MANAGEMENT AREA
Kentucky Dept. of Fish
and Wildlife Resources
Rte. 1, Box 84, La Center, KY 42056
(502) 224-2244 **BW, C, F, H, HR, PA**

PENNYRILE FOREST STATE RESORT PARK
Kentucky Dept. of Parks
20781 Pennyrile Lodge Rd.
Dawson Springs, KY 42408
(502) 797-3421 (information)
(800) 325-1711 (reservations)
BW, C, F, GS, H, I, L, MT, PA, S, T

PENNYRILE STATE FOREST
Kentucky Dept. of Forestry
PO Box 465, Madisonville, KY 42431-0465
(502) 825-6527
Primitive camping; vehicles on main-
tained roads only **BT, BW, C, CK, F, H,
HR, MB, MT, RC, S**

PILOT KNOB STATE NATURE PRESERVE
Kentucky State
Nature Preserves Commission
801 Schenkel Lane
Frankfort, KY 40601
(502) 573-2886 **BW, H, MT**

PINE MOUNTAIN STATE RESORT PARK
Kentucky Dept. of Parks
1050 State Park Rd., Pineville, KY 40977
(606) 337-3066; (800) 325-1712
**BW, C, GS, H, L,
MT, PA, S, T, TG**

QUIET TRAILS STATE
NATURE PRESERVE
Kentucky State
Nature Preserves Commission
801 Schenkel Lane
Frankfort, KY 40601
(502) 573-2886 **BW, H, MT**

RAVEN RUN NATURE SANCTUARY
Lexington-Fayette Urban County
Div. of Parks and Recreation
545 N. Upper St.
Lexington, KY 40508-1481
(606) 272-6105
Includes nature center; one handi-
capped-accessible trail; limited camping
BW, C, H, MT, PA, T, TG, XC

REDBIRD CREST TRAIL
Daniel Boone National Forest
Redbird Ranger District
HC 68, Box 65
Big Creek, KY 40914
(606) 598-2192
**BT, BW, C, F, H,
HR, MB, MT, XC**

RED RIVER GORGE
GEOLOGICAL AREA
Daniel Boone National Forest
Stanton Ranger District
705 West College Ave.
Stanton, KY 40380
(606) 663-2852 **BW, C, CK, F, H, HR, I,
MT, PA, RC, S, T, XC**

L Lodging	**PA** Picnic Areas	**RC** Rock Climbing	**TG** Tours, Guides
MB Mountain Biking	**RA** Ranger-led Activities	**S** Swimming	**XC** Cross-country Skiing
MT Marked Trails		**T** Toilets	

REELFOOT LAKE
NATIONAL WILDLIFE REFUGE
U.S. Fish and Wildlife Service
4343 Rte. 157, Union City, TN 38261
(901) 538-2481   **BW, CK, F, H**

SHELTOWEE TRACE NATIONAL
RECREATION TRAIL
Daniel Boone National Forest
1700 Bypass Rd, Winchester, KY 40391
(606) 745-3100
    BT, BW, C, F, H, HR, MB, MT, PA, XC

SHILLALAH CREEK WILDLIFE
MANAGEMENT AREA
Kentucky Dept. of Fish
and Wildlife Resources
1 Game Farm Rd., Frankfort, KY 40601
(606) 878-9595 (wildlife)
(606) 549-1332 (fish)
    Very limited access; 4WD trail only
    BW, F, H, RC

SIMON KENTON TRAIL
Kentucky Dept. of Parks
Capital Plaza Tower, 12th Floor
Frankfort, KY 40601
(502) 564-5410   **BW, C, MT**

SIX MILE ISLAND
STATE NATURE PRESERVE
Kentucky State Nature Preserves Commission
801 Schenkel Lane, Frankfort, KY 40601
(502) 573-2886   **BW**

SWAN LAKE WILDLIFE
MANAGEMENT AREA
Kentucky Dept. of Fish
and Wildlife Resources
Rte. 1, Box 84, La Center, KY 42056
(502) 224-2244   **BW, C, F, PA**

TAYLORSVILLE LAKE STATE PARK
Kentucky Dept. of Parks
1320 Park Rd., Mt. Eden, KY 40046
(502) 477-8713
    BW, F, H, HR, I, MT, PA, S, T

TAYLORSVILLE LAKE WILDLIFE
MANAGEMENT AREA
Kentucky Dept. of Fish
and Wildlife Resources
1 Game Farm Rd., Frankfort, KY 40601
(502) 564-4406
    BW, CK, F, H, HR, MT, S

TYGART STATE FOREST
Kentucky Div. of Forestry
249 W. 1st St., Morehead, KY 40351
(606) 784-7504
    BT, BW, C, CK, F, GS, H, HR, I,
    L, MB, MT, PA, RA, S, T, TG, XC

WINFORD WILDLIFE MANAGEMENT AREA
Kentucky Dept. of Fish
and Wildlife Resources
Rte. 1, Box 84, La Center, KY 42056
(502) 224-2244   **BW, F, H**

YELLOWBANK WILDLIFE
MANAGEMENT AREA
Kentucky Dept. of Fish
and Wildlife Resources
Rte. 1, Box 18
Stephensport, KY 40170
(502) 547-6856
    Primitive camping; caution during hunt-
    ing seasons, check with office
    BW, C, CK, F, H, HR, I, MB, MT

TENNESSEE

ANDERSON-TULLY WILDLIFE
MANAGEMENT AREA
Tennessee Wildlife Resources Agency
225 Martin Luther King Blvd.
State Office Bldg., Box 55
Jackson, TN 38301
(901) 635-7223
(901) 423-5725   **BW, C, F, H, HR**

APPALACHIAN NATIONAL SCENIC TRAIL
National Park Service
Appalachian Trail Conference
PO Box 807, Harpers Ferry, WV 25425-0807
(304) 535-6331
    No motorized vehicles; no horses; per-
    mits required for camping in some areas
    BW, C, F, H, MT, PA, RC, S, XC

BALD RIVER GORGE WILDERNESS
Cherokee National Forest
Tellico Ranger District
250 Ranger Station Rd.
Tellico Plains, TN 37385
(615) 253-2520   **BW, C, F, H, I, MT, S**

BAYS MOUNTAIN PARK
Kingsport Dept. of Parks and Recreation
853 Bays Mountain Park Rd.
Kingsport, TN 37660
(615) 229-9447

BT Bike Trails	**CK** Canoeing, Kayaking	**F** Fishing	**HR** Horseback Riding
BW Bird-watching	**DS** Downhill Skiing	**GS** Gift Shop	**I** Information Center
C Camping		**H** Hiking	

Includes nature center and planetarium; fishing limited to ages under 16 and over 65; no cooking in picnic areas

BT, BW, F, GS, H, I, MB, MT, PA, T, TG

BIG BONE CAVE STATE NATURAL AREA
Rock Island State Park
82 Beach Rd., Rock Island, TN 38581
(615) 686-2471
All tours through cave are ranger-led

BW, RA, TG

BIG CYPRESS TREE STATE NATURAL AREA
Tennessee State Parks
Kimery Rd., Greenfield, TN 38230
(901) 235-2700
Trail often flooded most of winter and spring; recommend call in advance to confirm conditions **BW, H, PA**

BIG HILL POND STATE PARK
Tennessee State Parks
Rte. 1, Box 150-C
Pocahontas, TN 38061
(901) 645-7967

BW, C, CK, F, GS, H, I, MT, PA, RA, T, TG

BIG RIDGE STATE PARK
Tennessee State Parks
1015 Big Ridge Park Rd.
Maynardsville, TN 37807
(615) 992-5523
Canoeing in park-owned canoes only

**BW, C, CK, F, GS,
H, I, L, MT, PA, S, T**

BIG SANDY UNIT, TENNESSEE NATIONAL WILDLIFE REFUGE
U.S. Fish and Wildlife Service
PO Box 849, Paris, TN 38242
(901) 642-2091 **BW, F, H, MT**

BIG SOUTH FORK NATIONAL RIVER AND RECREATION AREA
National Park Service
Rte. 3, Box 401, Oneida, TN 37841
(615) 879-3625

**BT, BW, C, CK, F, GS, H, HR, I, L, MB,
MT, PA, RA, RC, S, T, TG**

BLEDSOE CREEK STATE PARK
Tennessee State Parks
400 Zieglers Fort Rd., Gallatin, TN 37066
(615) 452-3706

BW, C, F, H, MT, PA, T

BURGESS FALLS STATE NATURAL AREA
Tennessee State Parks
4000 Burgess Falls Dr.
Sparta, TN 38583-8456
(615) 432-5312
Day use only **BW, F, H, I, MT, PA, T**

CARTER STATE NATURAL AREA
South Cumberland State Recreation Area
Rte. 1, Box 2196, Monteagle, TN 37356
(615) 924-2956
Day use only **BW, H, MT, RA**

CATOOSA WILDLIFE MANAGEMENT AREA
Tennessee Wildlife Resources Agency
216 East Penfield St.
Crossville, TN 38555
(615) 456-2479
Primitive camping in designated areas; closed to all but big-game hunters during hunting season

BW, C, CK, F, H, HR

CEDARS OF LEBANON STATE FOREST
Tennessee Div. of Forestry
5112 Murfreesboro Rd.
Lebanon, TN 37090
(615) 443-2768
Primitive camping; self-registration required **BT, BW, C, H, I, MB, MT, RA**

CEDARS OF LEBANON STATE PARK
Tennessee State Park
328 Cedar Forest Rd.
Lebanon, TN 37090
(615) 443-2769 **BW, C, GS, H, HR, I, L,
MB, MT, PA, RA, S, T**

CHEATHAM WILDLIFE MANAGEMENT AREA
Tennessee Wildlife Resources Agency
PO Box 40747, Nashville, TN 37204
(615) 781-6622
Primarily a hunting area; some roads closed during breeding, nesting, and rearing seasons **BW**

CHEROKEE NATIONAL FOREST
U.S. Forest Service
PO Box 2010, Cleveland, TN 37320
(615) 476-9700
Includes portion of the Appalachian Trail; ORV use in designated areas only

**BT, BW, C, CK, F, H, HR,
MB, MT, PA, RA, RC, S, T**

L	Lodging	**PA**	Picnic Areas	**RC**	Rock Climbing	**TG** Tours, Guides
MB	Mountain Biking	**RA**	Ranger-led Activities	**S**	Swimming	**XC** Cross-country Skiing
MT	Marked Trails			**T**	Toilets	

CHICKAMAUGA AND CHATTANOOGA NATIONAL MILITARY PARK
National Park Service
PO Box 2128, Fort Oglethorpe, GA 30742
(706) 866-9241   **H, HR, I, MT, T, TG**

CHICKASAW STATE PARK
Tennessee State Parks
20 Cabin Lane, Henderson, TN 38340
(901) 989-5141
                    **BT, BW, C, F, GS, H, HR, I,
                    L, MT, PA, RA, S, T**

**CHUCK SWANN
WILDLIFE MANAGEMENT AREA**
Tennessee Wildlife Resources Agency
3350 Sharps Chapel Rd.
Sharps Chapel, TN 37866
(615) 278-3248
    Primitive camping on perimeter; no
    horses in camping area
        BW, C, CK, F, H, HR, I, MB, PA, S

CRITICO CREEK WILDERNESS
Cherokee National Forest
Tellico Ranger District
250 Ranger Station Rd.
Tellico Plains, TN 37385
(615) 253-2520
                    BW, C, F, HR, I, MT, S

COKER CREEK SCENIC AREA
Cherokee National Forest
Hiwassee Ranger District
PO Box D, Etowah, TN 37331
(615) 263-5486
                    BW, C, F, H, MB, MT, PA, S

**CROSS CREEKS NATIONAL
WILDLIFE REFUGE**
U.S. Fish and Wildlife Service
643 Wildlife Rd., Dover, TN 37058
(615) 232-7477
    Day use only; tick repellant needed; no
    fires allowed   **BW, F, H, I, MT, TG**

CUMBERLAND CAVERNS
1437 Cumberland Caverns Rd.
McMinnville, TN 37110
(615) 668-4396
    Includes "God of the Mountain" drama-
    tization; open daily May through
    October, by appt. rest of year; admission
    fee; not handicapped-accessible
                    BW, GS, H, I, MT, PA, T, TG

**CUMBERLAND MOUNTAIN
STATE RUSTIC PARK**
Tennessee State Parks
Rte. 8, Box 322, Crossville, TN 38555
(615) 484-6138
    Cabins; boat rentals; no pets in cabins;
    no camping reservations, first come, first
    served   **BW, C, F, GS, II, I,
                            L, MT, PA, RA, S, T**

CYPRESS GROVE NATURE PARK
Jackson Recreation and Parks Dept.
400 South Highland Ave.
Jackson, TN 38301
(901) 425-8364
    Includes Aerie Trail Raptor Center, 5,000-
    ft. boardwalk, 2 lakes, observation tower
    group tours by appt.
                    BW, F, H, I, PA, T, TG

DAVID CROCKETT STATE PARK
Tennessee State Parks
PO Box 398, Lawrenceburg, TN 38464
(615) 762-9408
            BT, BW, C, F, GS, H, I, PA, RA, S, T

FALL CREEK FALLS STATE RESORT PARK
Tennessee State Parks
Rte. 3, Pikeville, TN 37367
(615) 881-5298 (info) (615) 881-5241 (res.)
    Cabins available; stay on trails
            **BT, BW, C, CK, F, GS, H, HR, I, L, MB,
                    MT, PA, RA, RC, S, T, TG**

FORT PILLOW STATE HISTORIC PARK
Tennessee State Park
Rte. 2, Box 109
Henning, TN 38041
(901) 738-5581
            BW, C, F, GS, H, I, MT, PA, RA, T

FOSTER FALLS TVA SMALL WILD AREA
South Cumberland State Recreation Area
Rte. 1, Box 2196
Monteagle, TN 37356
(615) 924-2956
            BW, C, F, H, MT, PA, RA, RC, S, T, TG

FROZEN HEAD STATE NATURAL AREA
Tennessee State Parks
964 Flat Fork Rd., Wartburg, TN 37887
(615) 346-3318
    Backcountry camping permits required
                **BW, C, F, GS, H, HR, I, MB,
                    MT, PA, RA, T, TG**

BT	Bike Trails	**CK**	Canoeing, Kayaking	**F**	Fishing	
BW	Bird-watching			**GS**	Gift Shop	
C	Camping	**DS**	Downhill Skiing	**H**	Hiking	

HR	Horseback Riding
I	Information Center

GEE CREEK WILDERNESS
Cherokee National Forest
Hiwassee Ranger District
PO Box D, Etowah, TN 37331
(615) 263-5486
Day use only **BW, H, MT**

GREAT SMOKY MOUNTAINS
NATIONAL PARK
National Park Service
107 Park Headquarters Rd.
Gatlinburg, TN 37738
(615) 436-1200
Includes portion of the Appalachian Trail
BW, C, F, GS, H, HR,
I, MT, PA, RA, T, TG

GRUNDY FOREST STATE NATURAL AREA
South Cumberland State Recreation Area
Rte. 1, Box 2196
Monteagle, TN 37356
(615) 924-2956 **BW, H, MT, PA, RA, S**

GRUNDY LAKES STATE PARK
South Cumberland State Recreation Area
Rte. 1, Box 2196, Monteagle, TN 37356
(615) 924-2956
Primitive camping, permit required
BW, C, F, H, MT, PA, RA, RC, S, T, TG

HARPETH SCENIC RIVER AND
NARROWS HISTORIC AREA
Montgomery Bell State Resort Park
PO Box 39, Burns, TN 37029
(615) 797-9052
Day use only **BW, CK, F, H, MT**

HATCHIE NATIONAL WILDLIFE REFUGE
U.S. Fish and Wildlife Service
4172 Rte. 76 S., Brownsville, TN 38012
(901) 772-0501
Roads closed seasonally due to flooding
BW, CK, F, I

HAWKINS COVE NATURAL AREA
South Cumberland State Recreation Area
Rte. 1, Box 2196, Monteagle, TN 37356
(615) 924-2956 **BW, H**

HUBBARD'S CAVE
The Nature Conservancy
Tennessee Field Office
2002 Richard Jones Rd., Ste. 304-C
Nashville, TN 37215
(615) 298-3111

Call in advance; large cave entrance is
gated and locked year-round to protect
hibernating bats **TG**

JOHN MUIR TRAIL
Big South Fork National River and
Recreation Area
Rte. 3, Box 401
Oneida, TN 37841
(615) 879-3625
Register before camping
BW, C, F, H, I, MT, S

LAKE ISOM NATIONAL WILDLIFE REFUGE
U.S. Fish and Wildlife Service
4343 Rte. 157
Union City, TN 38261
(901) 538-2481
Day use only; closed mid-October until
mid-March **BW, CK, F, H**

LAND BETWEEN THE LAKES
Tennessee Valley Authority
100 Van Morgan Drive
Golden Pond, KY 42211-9001
(502) 924-5602
BT, BW, C, CK, F, GS, H, HR, I,
MB, MT, PA, RA, S, T, TG

LAUREL HILL WILDLIFE
MANAGEMENT AREA
Tennessee Wildlife Resources Agency
PO Box 40747
Nashville, TN 37204
(615) 781-6622 **BW, F**

LICHTERMAN NATURE CENTER
Memphis Dept. of Parks and Recreation
5992 Quince Ave.
Memphis, TN 38119
(901) 767-7322
Admission fee; no pets
BW, H, I, MT, PA, T, TG

LONG HUNTER STATE PARK
Tennessee State Parks
2970 Hobson Pike
Hermitage, TN 37060
(615) 885-2422
Mountain biking permitted in dry weather only **BW, F, GS, H, I, MT, PA, S**

LOWER HATCHIE NATIONAL
WILDLIFE REFUGE
U.S. Fish and Wildlife Service

L	Lodging	**PA**	Picnic Areas	**RC**	Rock Climbing	**TG**	Tours, Guides
MB	Mountain Biking	**RA**	Ranger-led Activities	**S**	Swimming	**XC**	Cross-country Skiing
MT	Marked Trails			**T**	Toilets		

Rte. 3, Box 44 A, Ripley, TN 38063
(901) 635-7621
Includes Sunk Lake Natural Area
BW, CK, F, H

MEEMAN-SHELBY FOREST STATE PARK
Tennessee State Parks
Rte. 3, Box 10, Millington, TN 38053-5099
(901) 876-5215
Cabins available; lakes drained and
closed until 1997 or 1998
**BT, BW, C, GS, H,
HR, I, L, MT, PA, T**

**MONTGOMERY BELL
STATE RESORT PARK**
Tennessee State Parks
PO Box 39, Burns, TN 37029
(615) 797-9052 (visitor center)
(615) 797-3101 (inn)
**BW, C, CK, F, GS, H, I,
L, MT, PA, RA, S, T, TG**

NATCHEZ TRACE PARKWAY
National Park Service
2680 Natchez Trace Parkway
Tupelo, MS 38801
(601) 680-4025; (800) 305-7417
BW, C, CK, H, HR, I, MT, RA, S

**NATCHEZ TRACE
STATE RESORT PARK**
24845 Natchez Trace Rd.
Wildersville, TN 38388
(901) 968-3742 (info)
(901) 968-8176 (res)
Includes Natchez Trace State Forest
**BT, BW, C, CK, F, GS,
H, I, L, MT, PA, RA, S, T**

**NATHAN BEDFORD
FORREST STATE PARK**
Tennessee State Parks
Rte. 191, Eva, TN 38333
(901) 584-6356   **BW, C, F, GS, H, I, L,
MT, PA, RA, S, T, TG**

OBED WILD AND SCENIC RIVER
National Park Service
PO Box 429
Wartburg, TN 37887
(615) 346-6294
Primitive camping   **BW, C, CK, F,
H, I, PA, RC, S**

**OLD STONE FORT
ARCHAEOLOGICAL AREA**
Tennessee State Parks
732 Stone Fort Dr.
Manchester, TN 37355
(615) 723-5073
BW, C, F, GS, H, I, MT, PA, T, TG

PICKETT STATE PARK
Tennessee State Parks
Rte. 154
Jamestown, TN 38556
(615) 879-5821   **BT, BW, C, CK, F, GS, H,
HR, I, L, MT, PA, RA, RC, S, T**

**PRENTICE COOPER STATE FOREST AND
WILDLIFE MANAGEMENT AREA**
Tennessee Div. of Forestry
PO Box 160
Hixson, TN 37343
(615) 634-3091
Includes access to the Cumberland Trail;
prearranged group tours; primitive
camping; closed to all but big-game
hunters during hunting season
BW, C, F, H, HR, MB, MT, PA, RC, S

RADNOR LAKE STATE NATURAL AREA
Tennessee State Parks
1160 Otter Creek Rd.
Nashville, TN 37220
(615) 373-3467; (615) 377-1281
BW, GS, H, I, MT, RA, T, TG

**REFLECTION RIDING AND
CHATTANOOGA NATURE CENTER**
400 Garden Rd.
Chattanooga, TN 32419
(615) 821-9582 (Reflection Riding)
(615) 821-1160 (nature center)
BT, BW, GS, H, MT, RA, T

ROAN MOUNTAIN STATE PARK
Tennessee State Parks
Rte. 1, Box 236
Roan Mountain, TN 37687
(615) 772-3303   **BW, C, F, GS, H, I, L,
MT, PA, RA, S, T, TG, XC**

ROCK ISLAND STATE PARK
Tennessee State Parks
82 Beach Rd.
Rock Island, TN 38581
(615) 686-2471   **BW, C, CK, F, H, I, L,
MT, PA, RA, RC, S, T, TG**

BT Bike Trails	**CK** Canoeing, Kayaking	**F** Fishing	**HR** Horseback Riding
BW Bird-watching	**DS** Downhill Skiing	**GS** Gift Shop	**I** Information Center
C Camping		**H** Hiking	

SAVAGE GULF STATE NATURAL AREA
South Cumberland State Recreation Area
Rte. 1, Box 2196
Monteagle, TN 37356
BW, C, H, MT, PA, RA, RC, T, TG

SEWANEE NATURAL BRIDGE STATE NATURAL AREA
South Cumberland State Recreation Area
Rte. 1, Box 2196
Monteagle, TN 37356
(615) 924-2956   BW

SHELTOWEE TRACE NATIONAL RECREATION TRAIL
Daniel Boone National Forest
1700 Bypass Rd.
Winchester, KY 40391
(606) 745-3100   BT, BW, C, F, H, HR, MB, MT, PA, XC

SOUTH CUMBERLAND RECREATION AREA
Tennessee State Parks
Rte. 1, Box 2196
Monteagle, TN 37356
(615) 924-2956
BW, F, GS, H, I, MT, PA, RA, T, TG

UNAKA MOUNTAIN AUTO TOUR
Cherokee National Forest
Unaka Ranger District
1205 N. Main, Erwin, TN 37650
(615) 743-4452
30-mile self-guided auto tour   TG

UNAKA MOUNTAIN WILDERNESS
Cherokee National Forest
Unaka Ranger District
1205 N. Main
Erwin, TN 37650
(615) 743-4452
Primitive camping   BW, C, H, MT

VIRGIN FALLS POCKET WILDERNESS
Bowater, Inc., Southern Div. Woodlands
5020 Rte. 11 S.
Calhoun, TN 37309-0188
(615) 336-7424   H, MT

WARRIORS' PATH STATE PARK
Tennessee State Parks
PO Box 5026
Kingsport, TN 37663
(615) 239-8531; (615) 239-6786
BW, C, F, H, HR, I, MT, PA, RA, S, T, TG

WEST VIRGINIA

ALLEGHENY TRAIL
West Virginia Scenic Trails Association
633 West Virginia Ave.
Morgantown, WV 26505
(304) 296-5158
When on state property camp in authorized areas only
BW, C, F, H, MT, S

APPALACHIAN NATIONAL SCENIC TRAIL
National Park Service
Appalachian Trail Conference
PO Box 807
Harpers Ferry, WV 25425-0807
(304) 535-6331
No motorized vehicles; no horses; camping permits required in certain areas
BW, C, F, H, MT, PA, RC, S, XC

AUDRA STATE PARK
West Virginia Div.
of Natural Resources
Rte. 4, Box 564
Buckhannon, WV 26201
(304) 457-1162
BT, BW, C, CK, H, MB, PA, S, T

BABCOCK STATE PARK
West Virginia Div. of Natural Resources
HC 35, Box 150
Clifftop, WV 25831
(304) 438-3003; (800) 225-5982
Includes Glade Creek Grist Mill; open mid-April through October; cabins available
BT, BW, C, F, GS, H, HR, I, L, MB, MT, PA, RA, S, T

BEARTOWN STATE PARK
West Virginia Div. of
Natural Resources
HC 64, Box 189
Hillsboro, WV 24946
(304) 653-4254
Stay on boardwalk; climbing on rocks prohibited; tours by request
BW, H, I, PA, RA, T, TG

BEECH FORK STATE PARK
West Virginia Div. of Natural Resources
5601 Long Branch Rd.
Barboursville, WV 25504
(304) 522-0303   BT, BW, C, CK, F, H, I, MB, MT, PA, RA, T

L	Lodging	**PA**	Picnic Areas	**RC**	Rock Climbing
MB	Mountain Biking	**RA**	Ranger-led Activities	**S**	Swimming
MT	Marked Trails			**T**	Toilets

TG	Tours, Guides
XC	Cross-country Skiing

BERKELEY SPRINGS STATE PARK
West Virginia Div. of Natural Resources
121 S. Washington St.
Berkeley Springs, WV 25411
(304) 258-2711; (800) 225-5982
 Hours of operation vary; check
 with office   **GS, I, S, T**

BLACKWATER FALLS STATE PARK
West Virginia Div. of Natural Resources
PO Box 490
Davis, WV 26260
(304) 259-5216; (800) 225-5982
                BW, C, CK, F, GS, H, HR,
                I, L, MT, PA, RA, S, T, TG, XC

BLUE BEND RECREATION AREA
U.S. Forest Service
410 E. Main St.
White Sulphur Springs, WV 24986
(304) 536-2144
                BW, C, F, H, MT, PA, S, T

BLUESTONE NATIONAL SCENIC RIVER
National Park Service
PO Box 246, Glen Jean, WV 25846
(304) 465-0508
                BW, CK, F, H, MT, RA

BLUESTONE STATE PARK
West Virginia Div. of Natural Resources
HC 78, Box 3
Hinton, WV 25951
(304) 466-2805; (800) 225-5982
                BW, C, CK, F, GS, H, I,
                L, MT, PA, RA, S, T

CABWAYLINGO STATE FOREST
West Virginia Div. of Natural Resources
Rte. 1, Box 85, Dunlow, WV 25511
(304) 385-4255; (800) 225-5982
 Mountain biking on 4WD back roads
 BW, C, F, GS, H, I, L, MB, MT, PA, S, T

CACAPON STATE PARK
West Virginia Div.
of Natural Resources
Rte. 1, Box 304
Berkeley Springs, WV 25411
(304) 258-1022
 Pets on leashes during day; no pets
 overnight; cabins, rowboats, and pad-
 dleboats available; biking on roads only
                BW, F, GS, H, HR, I, L,
                MB, MT, PA, RA, S, T, TG, XC

CALVIN PRICE STATE FOREST
West Virginia Div. of Natural Resources
HC 82, Box 252, Marlinton, WV 24954-9550
(304) 799-4087
 Undeveloped area; primitive
 camping   **C, F**

CANAAN VALLEY RESORT
Guest Services, Inc.
HC 70, Box 330, Davis, WV 26260
(800) 622-4121
       C, DS, GS, H, I, L, MT, PA, S, T, TG, XC

CASS SCENIC RAILROAD STATE PARK
West Virginia Div. of Natural Resources
PO Box 107, Cass, WV 24927
(304) 456-4300; (800) 225-5982
 Fee charged for train ride and museum;
 cottages available   **B T, CK, F, GS, H, I,**
                L, MB, MT, PA, T, TG, XC

CATHEDRAL STATE PARK
West Virginia Div. of Natural Resources
Rte. 1, Box 370, Aurora, WV 26705
(304) 735-3771   **BT, BW, H, MB, MT,**
                PA, RA, T, TG, XC

CEDAR CREEK STATE PARK
West Virginia Div. of Natural Resources
Rte. 1, Box 9, Glenville, WV 26351
(304) 462-7158
                BT, BW, C, F, H, MB, MT, PA, S

CHIEF LOGAN STATE PARK
West Virginia Div. of Natural Resources
Logan, WV 25601
(304) 792-7125   **BW, C, F, H, HR**
                MT, PA, S, T

COOPERS ROCK STATE FOREST
West Virginia Div. of Natural Resources
Rte. 1, Box 270
Bruceton Mills, WV 26525
(304) 594-1561
 Tours by prearrangement
                BT, BW, C, F, GS, H,
                MB, MT, PA, RC, T, TG, XC

CRANBERRY GLADES BOTANICAL AREA
Monongahela National Forest
Gauley Ranger District
PO Box 110, Richwood, WV 26261
(304) 846-2695
 Sunday afternoon tours in summer
                BW, T, TG

BT	Bike Trails	**CK**	Canoeing, Kayaking	**F**	Fishing	**HR**	Horseback Riding
BW	Bird-watching			**GS**	Gift Shop		
C	Camping	**DS**	Downhill Skiing	**H**	Hiking	**I**	Information Center

CRANBERRY WILDERNESS
Monongahela National Forest
Gauley Ranger District
PO Box 110
Richwood, WV 26261
(304) 846-2695   **BW, C, H**

CRANESVILLE SWAMP
The Nature Conservancy of West Virginia
PO Box 3754
Charleston, WV 25337
(304) 345-4350
  Call field office for directions
                    BW, H, I, MT, XC

**DOLLY SODS WILDERNESS
AND SCENIC AREA**
Monongahela National Forest
Potomac Ranger District
HC 59, Box 240
Petersburg, WV 26847
(304) 567-2827 (Seneca Rocks visitor center)
(304) 257-4488 (Potomac Ranger Station)
  Primitive camping; pit toilets
                  BW, C, H, PA, T

GAUDINEER SCENIC AREA
Monongahela National Forest
Greenbrier Ranger District
PO Box 67, Bartow, WV 24920
(304) 456-3335   **BW, H, MT, PA, T, XC**

**GAULEY RIVER NATIONAL
RECREATION AREA**
National Park Service
PO Box 246
Glen Jean, WV 25846
(304) 465-050   **BW, C, CK, F, H, RC, T**

**GEORGE WASHINGTON AND JEFFERSON
NATIONAL FORESTS**
U.S. Forest Service
5162 Valley Point Pkwy.
Roanoke, VA 24019
(703) 265-6054   **BT, BW, C, CK, F, H,
HR, MB, MT, PA, S, T, XC**

GREENBRIER RIVER TRAIL
Superintendent, Watoga State Park
Rte. 1, Box 252
Marlinton, WV 24954
(304) 799-4087
  No motorized vehicles
            **BT, BW, C, CK, F, H,
HR, I, L, MB, MT, S, XC**

GREENBRIER STATE FOREST
West Virginia Div. of Natural Resources
HC 30, Box 154
Caldwell, WV 24925
(304) 536-1944; (800) 225-5982
  Cabins available   **BT, BW, C, GS, H, I, L,
MB, MT, PA, RA, S, T**

**HARPERS FERRY NATIONAL
HISTORICAL PARK**
National Park Service
PO Box 65
Harpers Ferry, WV 25425
(304) 535-6298
  Permit required for rock climbing
       H, I, MT, PA, RA, RC, T, TG

HAWKS NEST STATE PARK
West Virginia Div. of Natural Resources
PO Box 85, Ansted, WV 25812
(304) 658-5212; (800) 225-5982
            **BW, F, GS, H, I,
MT, PA, S, T, TG**

HOLLY RIVER STATE PARK
West Virginia Div. of Natural Resources
PO Box 70, Hacker Valley, WV 26222
(304) 493-6353; (800) 225-5982
  Lodging and camping offered April
  through November   **BW, C, F, GS, H,
L, MT, PA, RA, S, T**

ICE MOUNTAIN
The Nature Conservancy of West Virginia
PO Box 3754
Charleston, WV 25337
(304) 345-4350   **BW, H, MT**

KANAWHA STATE FOREST
West Virginia Div. of Natural Resources
Rte. 2, Box 285
Charleston, WV 25314
(304) 346-5654 (office)
(304) 342-3751 (stables)
  Call office for directions
             **BT, BW, C, H, HR,
I, MB, MT, PA, S, T,**

KUMBRABOW STATE FOREST
West Virginia Div. of Natural Resources
PO Box 65
Huttonsville, WV 26273
(304) 335-2219
(800) 225-5982
     BT, BW, C, F, H, MB, MT, PA, T, XC

L	Lodging	**PA**	Picnic Areas	**RC**	Rock Climbing	**TG** Tours, Guides
MB	Mountain Biking	**RA**	Ranger-led Activities	**S**	Swimming	**XC** Cross-country Skiing
MT	Marked Trails			**T**	Toilets	

LAKE SHERWOOD RECREATION AREA
U.S. Forest Service
410 E. Main St.
White Sulphur Springs, WV 24986
(304) 536-2144
BW, C, CK, F, H, MT, PA, S, T

LAUREL FORK NORTH WILDERNESS
Monongahela National Forest
Greenbrier Ranger District
PO Box 67
Bartow, WV 24920
(304) 456-3335
No motorized equipment except wheel-
chairs   BW, C, F, H, HR

LAUREL FORK SOUTH WILDERNESS
Monongahela National Forest
Greenbrier Ranger District
PO Box 67
Bartow, WV 24920
(304) 456-3335   BW, C, F, H, HR

LOST RIVER STATE PARK
West Virginia Div. of Natural Resources
HC 67, Box 24
Mathias, WV 26812
(304) 897-5372
Cabins available   BW, GS, H, HR, I,
L, MB, PA, RA, S, T

MONONGAHELA NATIONAL FOREST
U.S. Forest Service
200 Sycamore St.
Elkins, WV 26241-3962
(304) 636-1800
Includes the Cranberry Mountain and
Seneca Rocks visitor centers.
BT, BW, C, CK, DS, F, GS, H, HR, I, L,
MB, MT, PA, RA, RC, S, T, TG, XC

NEW RIVER GORGE NATIONAL RIVER
National Park Service
PO Box 246, Glen Jean, WV 25846
(304) 465-0508
Includes Thurmond Depot, Canyon Rim,
Grandview, and Hinton visitor center
BT, BW, C, CK, F, H, HR, I, MB, MT, PA,
RA, RC, T

NORTH BEND RAIL TRAIL
West Virginia Div. of Natural Resources
Rte. 1, Box 221
Cairo, WV 26337
(304) 643-2931   BT, H, HR, MB

NORTH BEND STATE PARK
West Virginia Div. of Natural Resources
Rte. 1, Box 221, Cairo, WV 26337
(304) 643-2931   BT, C, F, GS, H, HR, L,
MB, MT, PA, RA, S, T, TG

**OHIO RIVER ISLANDS NATIONAL
WILDLIFE REFUGE**
U.S. Fish and Wildlife Service
PO Box 1811, Parkersburg, WV 26102
(304) 422-0752
Day use only; no wheeled vehicles al-
lowed off trails   BT, BW, F, H, HR, MB, S

PANTHER STATE FOREST
West Virginia Div. of Natural Resources
PO Box 287
Panther, WV 24872
(304) 938-2252   C, F, H, MT, PA, S

PINNACLE ROCK STATE PARK
West Virginia Div. of Natural Resources
102 Tremon Park
Bluefield, WV 24701
(304) 589-5307
Day use only   H, MT, PA

PIPESTEM STATE PARK
West Virginia Div. of Natural Resources
PO Box 150, Pipestem, WV 25979
(304) 466-1800; (800) 225-5982
BW, C, F, GS, H, HR, I,
L, MB, MT, PA, RA, S, T, TG, XC

SENECA STATE FOREST
West Virginia Div. of Natural Resources
Rte. 1, Box 140, Dunmore, WV 24934
(304) 799-6213   C, CK, F, H, I,
L, MB, MT, PA, T

SMOKE HOLE
Monongahela National Forest
Potomac Ranger District
HC 59, Box 240, Petersburg, WV 26847
(304) 567-2827 (Seneca Rocks visitor center)
(304) 257-4488 (Potomac Ranger Station)
C, CK, F, H, I, MT, PA, RC, T

**SPRUCE KNOB/SENECA ROCKS NATIONAL
RECREATION AREA**
Monongahela National Forest
Potomac Ranger District
HC 59, Box 240, Petersburg, WV 26847
(304) 567-2827; (304) 257-4488
C, F, H, HR, I, MB, MT, PA, RC, T

BT Bike Trails	**CK** Canoeing, Kayaking	**F** Fishing	**HR** Horseback Riding
BW Bird-watching	**DS** Downhill Skiing	**GS** Gift Shop	**I** Information Center
C Camping		**H** Hiking	

TOMLINSON RUN STATE PARK
West Virginia Div. of Natural Resources
PO Box 97
New Manchester, WV 26256
(304) 564-3651   **BT, C, F, GS, H,
MT, PA, S, T**

TWIN FALLS STATE PARK
West Virginia Div. of Natural Resources
PO Box 1023, Mullens, WV 25882
(304) 294-4000; (800) 225-5982
   Includes Nature Center and Pioneer
   Farm; tours by prearrangement
                      **BT, BW, C, GS, H, I, L,
MB, MT, PA, RA, S, T, TG, XC**

TYGART LAKE STATE PARK
West Virginia Div. of Natural Resources
Rte. 1, Box 260, Grafton, WV 26354
(304) 265-3383 (park)
(304) 265-2320 (lodge)
(800) 225-5982   **BW, C, F, GS, H, I, L,
MT, PA, RA, S, T**

VALLEY FALLS STATE PARK
West Virginia Div. of Natural Resources
Rte. 6, Box, 244
Fairmont, WV 26554
(304) 367-2719
         BT, BW, CK, F, H, I, MB, PA, T, XC

WATOGA STATE PARK
West Virginia Div. of Natural Resources
HC 82, Box 252
Marlinton, WV 24954-9550
(304) 799-4087
   Cabins available
      **BT, BW, C, F, GS, H, HR, L, MB, MT, PA,
RA, S, T, TG, XC**

**WEST VIRGINIA STATE
WILDLIFE CENTER**
West Virginia Div. of Natural Resources
PO Box 38
French Creek, WV 26218
(304) 924-6211
         BW, F, GS, H, MT, PA, RA, T, TG

ABOVE: *In rural 1940 Kentucky, photographer Marion Post Wolcott discovered that rock slides were often the least of a traveler's challenges.*

L Lodging	**PA** Picnic Areas	**RC** Rock Climbing	**TG** Tours, Guides
MB Mountain Biking	**RA** Ranger-led Activities	**S** Swimming	**XC** Cross-country Skiing
MT Marked Trails		**T** Toilets	

INDEX

Numbers in **bold** indicate illustrations; numbers in **bold italics** indicate maps.